SECOND

Practical Application of
Entry-Level
HEALTH
EDUCATION
Skills

Michelyn Wilson Bhandari, DrPH, MPH, CPH
Eastern Kentucky University

Karen M. Hunter, MPH, RD, LD, CHES
Eastern Kentucky University

Kathleen Phillips, PhD, MCHES
Eastern Illinois University

EDITED BY

Bette Benewich Keyser, EdD, MS
Illinois State University

Marilyn J. Morrow, PhD, MS
Illinois State University

JONES & BARTLETT
LEARNING

World Headquarters
Jones & Bartlett Learning
5 Wall Street
Burlington, MA 01803
978-443-5000
info@jblearning.com
www.jblearning.com

Jones & Bartlett Learning books and products are available through most bookstores and online booksellers. To contact Jones & Bartlett Learning directly, call 800-832-0034, fax 978-443-8000, or visit our website, www.jblearning.com.

Substantial discounts on bulk quantities of Jones & Bartlett Learning publications are available to corporations, professional associations, and other qualified organizations. For details and specific discount information, contact the special sales department at Jones & Bartlett Learning via the above contact information or send an email to specialsales@jblearning.com.

Practical Application of Entry-Level Health Education Skills, Second Edition is an independent publication and has not been authorized, sponsored, or otherwise approved by the owners of the trademarks or service marks referenced in this product.

This publication is designed to provide accurate and authoritative information in regard to the Subject Matter covered. It is sold with the understanding that the publisher is not engaged in rendering legal, accounting, or other professional service. If legal advice or other expert assistance is required, the service of a competent professional person should be sought.

Production Credits
Publisher: Cathleen Sether
Executive Editor: Shoshanna Goldberg
Editorial Assistant: Sean Coombs
Production Manager: Julie Champagne Bolduc
Production Editor: Jessica Steele Newfell
Senior Marketing Manager: Andrea DeFronzo
VP, Manufacturing and Inventory Control: Therese Connell
Composition: Laserwords Private Limited, Chennai, India
Cover and Title Page Design: Scott Moden
Cover, Title Page, and Chapter-Opening Image: © Filipchuk Oleg Vasiliovich/ShutterStock, Inc.
Printing and Binding: Courier Companies
Cover Printing: Courier Companies

To order this product, use ISBN: 978-1-4496-8389-4

Library of Congress Cataloging-in-Publication Data
Practical application of entry-level health education skills / edited by Bette Benewich Keyser, Marilyn J. Morrow.–2nd ed.
    p. ; cm.
Rev. ed. of: Practicing the application of health education skills and competencies / [edited by] Bette B. Keyser . . . [et al.]. c1997.
    Includes bibliographical references and index.
    ISBN 978-1-4496-2106-3—ISBN 1-4496-2106-6
    I. Keyser, Bette Benewich. II. Morrow, Marilyn J. III. Practicing the application of health education skills and competencies.
    [DNLM: 1. Health Education–Problems and Exercises. WA 18.2]
    613.076–dc23
                                2012010750
6048

Printed in the United States of America
16 15 14 13 12   10 9 8 7 6 5 4 3 2 1

Contents

Contents

Letter

Contents

Contents

Chapter 5   Administer and Manage Health Education...............155

Contents

Preface

This second edition of *Practical Application of Entry-Level Health Education Skills* was written in response to the changes and developments in health education professional preparation programs. This text addresses findings of the National Health Educator Job Analysis—2010 (HEJA 2010) study reflected in *A Competency-Based Framework for Health Education Specialists—2010*, published by the National Commission for Health Education Credentialing, Inc. (NCHEC), the Society for Public Health Education (SOPHE), and the American Association for Health Education (AAHE). The HEJA 2010 study findings resulted in the identification of new and/or expanded competencies in the areas of consultative relationships, ethics, influencing policy, partnership development, promoting the health education profession, and training. Additionally, recommendations from the HEJA 2010 suggested that professional development activities should use all of the responsibilities, competencies, and sub-competencies and that these components should serve as a basis for assuring the quality of professional preparation programs among accrediting bodies in the profession (AAHE, NCHEC, and SOPHE, 2010). Thus, this text includes competency-based application activities that can be used across the curriculum in health education professional preparation programs to provide an opportunity for students to practice professional skills in the Seven Areas of Responsibility as set forth in the HEJA 2010.

Each of the seven chapters in this text corresponds with one of the Seven Areas of Responsibility. Each chapter contains at least one activity for each entry-level sub-competency that corresponds with the area of responsibility. Each activity contains elements of knowledge and skills that, in partnership, provide a richer learning experience while preparing students as entry-level health education specialists.

This edition, along with the *First Edition,* is based on the authors' beliefs that pedagogy of hands-on learning, student-centered learning, and learning by doing is necessary for professional skill development. Active learning provides the student with the confidence to apply skills successfully as an entry-level health education specialist.

The connection between learning content and practicing skills and competencies is made clear in the activities in this text. For example, an activity designed to address sub-competency 1.6.1, "Determine the Extent of Available Health Education Programs, Interventions, and Policies," is titled "Community Health Status Indicators Data of Selected Counties." This activity combines the student's knowledge of prevention practices and ability to navigate a U.S. Department of Health and Human Services tool with the purpose of identifying the availability of preventive health services in a selected target county and then comparing the utilization patterns with a peer county.

The 148 sub-competency-based activities in this text are not likely to be completed within a single course; they should instead be integrated across the curriculum in health education professional preparation programs. The combination of student-centered, skill-building activities over several semesters or quarters will benefit students' professional growth in skills and competencies. Upon completion of the hands-on, student-centered activities, students will realize an increase in confidence in their ability to perform the Seven Areas of Responsibility of an entry-level health education specialist across diverse work settings.

Highlights of the *Second Edition* include:

- A total of 148 activities that correlate with a responsibility, competency, and sub-competency from *A Competency-Based Framework for Health Education Specialists—2010* (NCHEC, SOPHE, and AAHE, 2010).
- Each of the seven chapters is devoted to the primary responsibilities, competencies, and sub-competencies of an education specialist.

- Chapter introductions provide an overview of the concepts, models, and theories significant to various competencies for the chapter, skills that students will be practicing through hands-on activities, and an explanation of the learning content that can be infused into the activities.

- Every activity clearly identifies the title of the sub-competency addressed, provides a learning objective, outlines directions for completing the activity, and provides resources needed to complete the activity.

- Case studies provide students with views of different issues in a variety of health-education settings.

- Students are given the opportunity to apply current technology to various activities and health-education settings.

- Self-assessment tools measure the student's ability and confidence to perform the skill/competency.

- Relevant and diverse websites increase knowledge of key content areas and/or provide resources to increase skills.

- Instructor resources include ideas for instructors to introduce and conduct the activity and distinguish between activities most appropriate for use in major classes and those that are more appropriate for out-of-class experiences, such as service learning, student teaching, or internships.

An additional benefit of completing the activities in this text is student documentation of completed skills. Evidence of the completion of competency-based activities will be appropriate to include in a professional portfolio, an educational tool that many new graduates are finding beneficial in the job market. Such evidence also provides a practical method of documenting student-demonstrated skills in meeting criteria for program assessment, accreditation, or approval purposes.

The authors and editors of this edition of *Practical Application of Entry-Level Health Education Skills* have more than 100 years of combined experience teaching community health, school health education, and public health students. The authors and editors, over the course of their many teaching years, have prepared students for careers in health education and enhanced students' processional growth by encouraging them to attend state and national health education conferences, present at conferences, apply for scholarships, submit applications for awards and graduate school, participate in Eta Sigma Gamma, prepare to take the Certified Health Education Specialist examination, and, as alumni, serve on advisory councils and speak to undergraduates. The professional growth and competence obtained by completing the skills-based activities in this text will prepare students for their culminating field experiences and readiness for employment as entry-level education specialists.

References

American Association for Health Education, National Commission for Health Education Credentialing, and Society for Public Health Education (AAHE, NCHEC, and SOPHE, 2010). (2010). *Health educator job analysis—2010: Executive summary and recommendations*. Retrieved from http://www.nchec.org/_files/_items/nch-mr-tab3-193/docs/health%20educator%20job%20 analysis%20ex%20summary-final-2-19-10.pdf

National Commission for Health Education Credentialing, Society for Public Health Education, and American Association for Health Education (NCHEC, SOPHE, and AAHE). (2010). *A competency-based framework for health education specialists—2010.*

To the Instructor

Practical Application of Entry-Level Health Education Skills, Second Edition is a tool that faculty can use to engage students in practicing the skills necessary to meet the current competencies and sub-competencies of the Seven Areas of Responsibility identified in the 2010 Health Education Job Analysis study. Faculty will select from 148 activities to use in a professional preparation program. Some activities are self-contained and can be completed by the students independently after an introduction to the sub-competency. Other activities require additional support from the instructor or can be accomplished within out-of-class experiences such as service learning or internships. Clear directions, additional support, and suggestions are provided in the instructor ancillaries for each activity.

Instructor resources also include student assessments. The Unit Assessment is designed as a self-assessment for students to rate their abilities and confidence in performing each Responsibility before and again after completion of the chapter activities. The Activity Rubric Assessment is intended for instructors to administer at their discretion, and this rubric assessment measures the quality of student performance upon completion and submission of any activity to the instructor. Additionally, the instructor resources include at least one multiple choice or short answer assessment question for each of the 148 activities.

The activities in this text will supplement the traditional approach of teaching (e.g., lectures, worksheets, readings) by enabling each student to actually practice professional skills in the Seven Areas of Responsibility. It is recommended that professional preparation program faculty choose to integrate the activities throughout a curriculum by selecting appropriate activities that best fit course objectives and student outcomes. The text will provide a practical method for student documentation of demonstrated skills essential for program assessment, approval, or accreditation.

Acknowledgments

The authors gratefully acknowledge the important contributions of the following individuals:

Faculty from the Department of Health Studies at Eastern Illinois University for their creative and innovative ideas and willingness to share them; among others, this includes:

- Julie Dietz, PhD
- Misty Roads, PhD
- Anita Sego, MS
- Lauri DeRuiter-Willems, MS

Shoshanna Goldberg, Executive Editor, Sean Coombs, Editorial Assistant, and Jessica Newfell, Production Editor, at Jones & Bartlett Learning for advising, supporting, and assisting the authors and editors in multiple ways during completion of this text

Sandra McBride, Office Manager, Department of Health Sciences, Illinois State University, for editing, organization, and encouragement

Meagan Schorr, graduate of the Department of Health Sciences, Illinois State University, for providing an invaluable student's perspective

The authors also would like to thank the following reviewers for their feedback and insight during the development of this text:

Carl I. Fertman, PhD, MCHES, University of Pittsburgh

Joyce Kelly Graves, PhD, DNSc, RN, University of California, Los Angeles

Laura Nabors, PhD, ABPP, University of Cincinnati

Mary C. Schutten, PED, Grand Valley State University

Shawna D. Shane, EdD, Emporia State University

Virginia Verhoff, PhD, Western Connecticut State University

Assess Needs, Assets, and Capacity for Health Education

INTRODUCTION

This chapter introduces the needs assessment component of program planning through a total of 28 activities that address 34 entry-level sub-competencies in Area of Responsibility I.

Students will be exposed to a variety of planning models such as PRECEDE–PROCEED and logic models as well as behavior change theories such as health belief, social cognitive, and diffusions models. Activities will provide opportunities to explore available databases and resources like ERIC and the U.S. National Library of Medicine. These activities will require students to expand their knowledge on topics ranging from college relationship violence, personal safety, Internet use for bullying, obesity, and tobacco prevention among diverse cultures in both school and community settings.

Activities will assist students in understanding the distinction of primary and secondary data and recognize how health educators can use both qualitative and quantitative data in the needs assessment process. Students will identity the benefits of focus groups, nominal group method, key informant interviews, direct observation, and other methods in specific situations when needs assessment data is required. Students will be challenged to analyze factors that enhance or hinder the process of health education and finally make recommendations for health education programming based upon needs assessment findings.

Students will practice using a variety of interactive tools that can be used to evaluate Internet health information, explore community health status indicators, assess needs and resources of a community, develop steps in creating and maintaining a coalition or partnership, analyze comprehensive school health curriculum, and prioritize school health needs. They will be asked to use technologies, such as podcasts and presentation software, to complete some activities.

For this text, please go to the student companion website at **go.jblearning.com/PracticalApp** to complete activities using e-templates, and then pass your completed activities to your instructor for review or grading.

COMPETENCY 1.1 PLAN ASSESSMENT PROCESS

1.1.1 Identify Existing and Needed Resources to Conduct Assessments

Title Needs Assessment Models

Objective The student will be able to describe and apply models of needs assessment to specific situations.

Directions

Listed next are four needs assessment models that have been identified in the literature (Issel, 2009).

    a. Epidemiological model
    b. Public health model
    c. Social model
    d. Asset model

1. Review material on the four types of models for needs assessment (epidemiological model, public health model, social model, and asset model). The Community Tool Box listed in **Student Resource** (KU Work Group, 2010a, 2010b, 2010c) is an excellent resource to help with this activity. On the main page of the Community Tool Box, click on the Table of Contents. Use Chapter 3, Section 2, "Understanding and Describing the Community," Chapter 3, Section 4, "Collecting Information About the Problem," and Chapter 3, Section 8, "Identifying Community Assets and Resources."
2. Complete **Table 1.1.1-1**. The completed table will help with understanding the focus, scope of information collection, and advantages and disadvantages of using the different types of needs assessment models.

Table 1.1.1-1 Comparison of Four Types of Assessment Models

Assessment Model	What Is the Focus of This Model?	What Assessment Questions Does This Model Ask?	Advantages	Disadvantages
Epidemiological model				
Public health model				
Social model				
Asset model				

Adapted from Issel, M. (2009). *Health program planning and evaluation: A practical systematic approach for community health* (2nd ed.). Sudbury, MA: Jones & Bartlett Learning.

Student Resource
The Community Tool Box
http://ctb.ku.edu/en/default.aspx

References

Issel, L. M. (2009). *Health program planning and evaluation: A practical, systematic approach for community health* (2nd ed.). Sudbury, MA: Jones & Bartlett Learning.

KU Work Group for Community Health and Development. (2010a). Collecting information about the problem. In: *The community tool box* (Chapter 3, Section 4). Lawrence: University of Kansas. Retrieved from http://ctb.ku.edu/en/tablecontents/section_1022.aspx

KU Work Group for Community Health and Development. (2010b). Identifying community assets and resources. In *The community tool box* (Chapter 3, Section 8). Lawrence: University of Kansas. Retrieved from http://ctb.ku.edu/en/tablecontents/section_1043.aspx

KU Work Group for Community Health and Development. (2010c). Understanding and describing the community. In: *The community tool box* (Chapter 3, Section 2). Lawrence: University of Kansas. Retrieved from http://ctb.ku.edu/en/tablecontents/section_1020.aspx

1.1.3 Apply Theory and Models to Develop Assessment Strategies

Title Planning Assessment Strategies Using Models as a Guide

Objective The student will be able to develop a plan for assessment using models of assessment as a guide.

Directions

1. Since health and health behavior are influenced by multiple factors (e.g., families, schools, employers, social networks, organizations, communities, laws/policies, and societies), the assessment strategy must include collection of data that answers what is happening and why it is happening. Decide if each of the four types of models presented in **Sub-competency 1.1.1** is designed to answer the following questions:
   a. What is happening?
   b. Why is it happening?
2. Prepare to justify responses for each question.
3. Develop an assessment plan for each of the following *scenarios* using one or more of the four types of assessment models. Record responses in **Table 1.1.3-1**.

Scenario 1

Assume the role of school health curriculum coordinator. The school board has asked for information to determine if an after-school program for the community is needed. Find out what the main concerns of the community are; the best times and places to offer the program; how much, if any, should be charged for the program; and the specific target group that would benefit the most from the program.

Scenario 2

A local community is experiencing an increase in the number of migrant and seasonal farm workers. A county health educator of a local health education team wants to make sure the health needs of the workers and their families will be met and to determine if the community has the resources to handle the new residents.

Scenario 3

The health officials of a local Native American tribe have expressed concerns about the health of their adolescents on the reservation. Assume the role of a recently employed school health educator for the reservation schools who has been asked to assist with a needs assessment to identify the health issues and problems of the youth living on the reservation.

Reference

Issel, M. (2009). *Health program planning and evaluation: A practical systematic approach for community health* (2nd ed.). Sudbury, MA: Jones & Bartlett Learning.

Table 1.1.3-1 Assessment Data Collection Plan Using Assessment Models

Purpose of Assessment	Types of Data to Be Collected	Assessment Model Used
Scenario 1		
What is happening?		
Why is it happening?		
Scenario 2		
What is happening?		
Why is it happening?		
Scenario 3		
What is happening?		
Why is it happening?		

Adapted from Issel, M. (2009). *Health program planning and evaluation: A practical systematic approach for community health* (2nd ed.). Sudbury, MA: Jones & Bartlett Learning.

1.1.4 Develop Plans for Data Collection, Analysis, and Interpretation

1.1.6 Integrate Research Designs, Methods, and Instruments into Assessment Plans

Title Planning for Data Collection and Analysis

Objective The student will be able to develop a plan for data collection and analysis that integrates methods to produce valid data.

Directions

1. Read the following *scenario*.
   Imagine a health educator has been assigned to a community health assessment planning group investigating obesity and its associated behavioral and nonbehavioral contributors. The only available data for the community are those showing the overall prevalence of obesity. However, the group wants to collect data from different subpopulations (i.e., whites, blacks, Hispanics, children, and adults) in order to identify disparities in obesity prevalence. Assume that multiple approaches (quantitative and/or qualitative methods using primary and/or secondary data) may be used based on program needs. The timeline for completion of the assessment from beginning to end is 3 months.
2. Review material provided by the course instructor on methods of collecting needs assessment data, and then complete **Table 1.1.4-1**.
3. Use completed data collection plan in **Table 1.1.4-1** and material provided by your course instructor to record in **Table 1.1.4-2** data collection issues that are threats to producing valid data and solutions to assuring data are valid and unbiased.

Table 1.1.4-1 Data Collection and Analysis Plan

Assessment Question	Information Needed	From Whom	How Collected (Quantitative or Qualitative; Primary or Secondary)	When Collected (General Timeline)	Analysis (How Results for Questions Will Be Produced)

Adapted from Hodges, B. C., & Videto, D. M. (2011). *Assessment and planning in health programs* (2nd ed.). Sudbury, MA: Jones & Bartlett Learning.

Table 1.1.4-2 Data Collection Methods: Investigating Threats and Solutions to Achieve Quality Data

Identify Threats to Producing Valid Data	Solutions to Address Threats to Validity	Identify Sources of Bias	Solutions to Limit Bias

Adapted from Hodges, B. C., & Videto, D. M. (2011). *Assessment and planning in health programs* (2nd ed.). Sudbury, MA: Jones & Bartlett Learning.

4. Adjust, as needed, the data collection and analysis plan in **Table 1.1.4-1** to ensure that the data collected is valid and unbiased.

Reference

Hodges, B. C., & Videto, D. M. (2011). *Assessment and planning in health programs* (2nd ed.). Sudbury, MA: Jones & Bartlett Learning.

COMPETENCY 1.2 ACCESS EXISTING INFORMATION AND DATA RELATED TO HEALTH

1.2.1 Identify Sources of Data Related to Health

Title Searching the Internet

Objectives
1. The student will be able to identify sources of data related to health on the Internet.
2. The student will be able to analyze the type of data available in Internet sources.

Directions
1. Access three Internet sources that provide data related to health and give an overview. The instructor will provide a list of valid and reliable sources that health educators often use for data. These sources contain enormous amounts of data so it is important to spend time reviewing what is available.
2. Complete **Table 1.2.1-1** after reviewing each source.

Table 1.2.1-1 Internet Health Data Sources

Name of Data Source	URL	Data Content Categories Available	One Example of Data Type Found
Environmental Protection Agency[a]	www.epa.gov	Sciences and technology, laws and regulations, popular topics, information by location	Toxicity and exposure assessment for children's health (TEACH database)
1.			
2.			
3.			

[a]Environmental Protection Agency. (n.d.). *Home page.* Retrieved from http://epa.gov

1.2.2 Critique Sources of Health Information Using Theory and Evidence from the Literature

Title Critiquing Sources of Health Information

Objective The student will be able to list procedures for critiquing health information sources.

Directions

1. Go to the U.S. National Library of Medicine web page (lm.nih.gov/medlineplus), and click on Videos and Cool Tools. Then click on the Evaluation Health Information button.
2. Complete the tutorial called, "Evaluating Internet Health Information: A Tutorial from the National Library of Medicine."
3. List in **Table 1.2.2-1** the nine questions suggested in the tutorial to ask when visiting a website for health information.
4. Select and conduct an Internet search on any health topic, issue, or product of interest as a prospective health educator. Then select one website from the search findings to review.
5. Complete **Table 1.2.2-1** by answering the nine questions from the tutorial for the website selected and reviewed.
6. Write concluding statements in the space below Q9 describing the quality of this website for health information.

Table 1.2.2-1 Tutorial Questions to Critique a Health Information Website

Name and URL of site:	
Tutorial Questions	**Responses to Questions for Site**
Q1	
Q2	
Q3	
Q4	
Q5	
Q6	

(continues)

Table 1.2.2-1 Tutorial Questions to Critique a Health Information Website *(continued)*

Q7	
Q8	
Q9	
Concluding statement:	

Reference

Medline Plus, National Library of Medicine. (2010, July). *Evaluating Internet health information: A tutorial from the National Library of Medicine.* Retrieved from http://www.nim.nih.gov/medlineplus/webeval/eval.html

1.2.3 Select Valid Sources of Information about Health

Title Valid or Not Valid Source

Objective The student will be able select and justify valid sources of health-related information available on the Internet.

Directions

1. Review the National Library of Medicine criteria for identifying valid websites available in **Activity 1.2.2**.
2. Conduct an Internet search to find sites that provide health-related information.
3. Apply the National Library of Medicine criteria to each site to find two sites that meet:
   a. Five or more of the nine criteria
   b. Four or fewer of the nine criteria
4. Write a separate paragraph summarizing the analysis for each Internet site found in **Step 3**. Include in the paragraph the following:
   a. Name and URL of the website
   b. Findings of applying the National Library of Medicine criteria to the website
   c. Reference for the website in APA style or style preferred by the instructor

Student Resource

American Psychological Association website
http://www.apastyle.org

Reference

Medline Plus, National Library of Medicine. (2010, July). *Evaluating Internet health information: A tutorial from the National Library of Medicine*. Retrieved from http://www.nim.nih.gov/medlineplus/webeval/eval.htm

1.2.4 Identify Gaps in Data Using Theories and Assessment Models

Title Community Health Status Indicators: What Is Missing from the Selected County's Data?

Objective The student will be able to use the PRECEDE–PROCEED model to identify gaps in data from the community health status indicators for a community.

Directions

1. The U.S. Department of Health and Human Services (2009) maintains a website (communityhealth .hhs.gov) containing community health status indicators (CHSI). Data are available for every county in every state in the United States. Use of the PRECEDE component of the PRECEDE–PROCEED model helps identify missing information to complete a community needs assessment. Go to communityhealth.hhs.gov and select a state and county. Then click on the Display Data button.
2. Select the Print Full Report link to bring up a file. Save the file to the desktop for later use.
3. Go to the Community Toolbox at ctb.ku.edu/en/default.aspx (KU Work Group, 2010). Click on the Table of Contents button, select Chapter 2, and then select Section 2 for a thorough review of the model.
4. Use the first three phases of the PRECEDE model to identify and collect data available in the community health status indicators for developing a program to reduce the incidence of obesity in the chosen community. Enter data in **Table 1.2.4-1**.
5. Based on the data review of the selected community, also use **Table 1.2.4-1** to make suggestions for collecting missing data that is key to developing a program to reduce the incidence of obesity.

Table 1.2.4-1 PRECEDE Model Phases for Selected Community Data

Community health status indicators data for obesity reduction County_____ State_____		
PRECEDE Phases	**Data Present**	**Data Needed**
Phase 1: Social assessment Quality of Life		

Phase 2: Epidemiologic assessment
  Health
  Genetics
  Behavior
  Environment		

Phase 3: Education and ecological assessment
  Predisposing
  Reinforcing
  Enabling		

Suggestions for collecting missing data:		

References

Department of Health and Human Services. (2009). *Community health status indicators.* 2009. Retrieved from http://www.communityhealth.hhs.gov/homepage.aspx?j=1

KU Work Group for Community Health and Development. (2010). PRECEDE–PROCEED. In: *The community tool box* (Chapter 2, Section 2). Lawrence, KS: University of Kansas. Retrieved from http://ctb.ku.edu/en/tablecontents/section_1008.aspx

1.2.5 Establish Collaborative Relationships and Agreements that Facilitate Access to Data

Title Understanding Data Policies

Objective The student will be able to describe how to obtain access to data by following an agency data use policy.

Directions

1. Assume the role of a health educator who is working as part of a health education team to conduct a needs/resource assessment of local public health departments. The health educator needs to provide a regional comparison of local health department funding, workforce, activities, and services and has identified the National Profile of Local Health Departments Study Series as a good source of data for conducting this assessment. This data is available from the National Association of County and City Health Officials (NACCHO) but requires a data use agreement in order to access the data. The health educator must present an outline of the steps to obtain access to the data for the health education team that is conducting the needs/resource assessment.

2. Access the website for NACCHO to learn how to obtain data from the National Profile of Local Health Departments Study Series. See **Student Resource** for the URL. First, conduct a search using the phrase, "Profile Data Use Policy." Next, locate and click on the link to Data Requests and Technical Documentation, and then locate the "Profile Data Request Application."

3. Prepare an outline of the steps to obtain access to the data by answering the following questions about NACCHO's data use policy as outlined in the "Profile Data Request Application."
   a. What is the fee for obtaining the data?
   b. Can the fee be reduced or waived? If yes, what must be provided by the person making the request?
   c. Does NACCHO allow access to data that identifies local health departments? If yes, what must be provided by the person making the request?
   d. What information about the use of the data (e.g., description of planned research) must be provided by the person making the request?
   e. List the provisions for using the data. For example, any publication of the data must acknowledge NACCHO.
   f. Is a signature required?

Student Resource

National Association of County and City Health Officials
http://www.naccho.org

1.2.6 Conduct Searches of Existing Databases for Specific Health-Related Data

Title ERIC Is Not Just a Boy's Name

Objective The student will be able to apply the skills of accessing ERIC documents to develop programs and other health education materials in specific health topics.

Directions

This activity utilizes the ERIC (Education Resources Information Center; U.S. Department of Education, n.d.) database available through university libraries and Internet browsers at eric.ed.gov. ERIC includes journal articles and other documents related to education.

Part 1

1. Find the ERIC home page (eric.ed.gov) and select one of the following age groups.
   a. Preschool children
   b. Elementary students
   c. Middle school students
   d. High school students
2. Use the ERIC thesaurus and type in the selected group to see how ERIC defines (scope note) that descriptor. Broader terms (BT), narrower terms (NT), and related terms (RT) will be provided also, if available.
3. Select one of the following topic areas: Health promotion, special health problems, or communicable diseases. Use the thesaurus again to define that descriptor and terms.
4. List the selected student age category and topic area in **Table 1.2.6-1**. For each term, provide the scope note (SN), one broader term (BT), a narrower term (NT), and three related terms (RT) as provided by the thesaurus.
5. Write in n/a if any information is not available. Do not leave blanks.

Part 2

1. Imagine making a presentation on either Internet bullying in middle school children or problems related in obese high school students. For this assignment, use only journal articles and books.

Table 1.2.6-1 ERIC Descriptors

Types of descriptors for age category and topic area
Term 1 (age category)_____
SN_____
BT_____ NT_____
RT_____
Term 2 (topic area)_____
SN_____
BT_____ NT_____
RT_____

2. Select one of the two presentation topics and conduct an ERIC advanced search for journals and books published 1990 or later. This advanced search is available through either a link on the home page or by positioning the cursor over the Search ERIC tab and selecting Advanced Search from the tab menu.

3. Record the student age category in the first blank and the topic area in the second blank, creating a search combining the two descriptors.

4. On the same page, check boxes to indicate that only journals and books should be used, and select 1990 from the drop list to indicate that only journals and books published in 1990 or later should be included. Click on the Search button and wait for ERIC to provide the results.

5. Choose five articles and use the My Clipboard option by clicking Add across from the title of each text to store the articles on a temporary space. Scroll to the top of the screen and click on the clipboard icon to see your list. Print results.

Reference

U.S. Department of Education, Institute of Education Science (n.d.). *Education Resources Information Center (ERIC)*. Retrieved from http://www.eric.ed.gov

COMPETENCY 1.3 COLLECT QUANTITATIVE AND/OR QUALITATIVE DATA RELATED TO HEALTH

1.3.1 Collect Primary and/or Secondary Data

Title Distinguishing Types of Data Collection: Who, What, When, Where, and Why

Objectives

1. The student will be able to distinguish among primary, secondary, qualitative, and quantitative data.
2. The student will be able to relate human subjects/institutional review board protocols to primary data collection.

Directions

1. Review material provided by the course instructor to complete **Table 1.3.1-1**. The completed table will focus on differences between primary and secondary data as well as qualitative and quantitative data.
2. To collect primary data, it is necessary to understand human subjects and institutional review board (IRB) protocols. Complete **Table 1.3.1-2** concerning human subjects and IRB to organize key concepts.

Table 1.3.1-1 Defining and Comprehending Four Types of Data

Type of Data	Definition	How Health Educators Can Use Data	Example
Primary			
Secondary			
Qualitative			
Quantitative			

Table 1.3.1-2 Human Subjects and IRB

Topics	What Does This Mean?	When Do Health Educators Use Human Subjects?	Why Do Health Educators Need to Submit Protocols?
Research involving human subjects			
Institutional review board (IRB) protocols			

1.3.2 Integrate Primary Data with Secondary Data

Title Setting Priorities: Integration of Primary and Secondary Data Sets

Objective The student will be able to use both primary and secondary data to formulate a report with recommendations for needed health services and education programs.

Directions

1. Review a fictitious data set provided by the instructor that represents findings of a recent needs assessment done at College XYZ. The fictitious data will be provided in a table identical to **Table 1.3.2-1**.
2. Use data in **Step 1** as primary data—that is, data collected directly from an individual about a certain topic or subject. A questionnaire is a typical means of collecting college health assessment data from students.
3. Access the Internet site for American College Health Association-National College Health Assessment (www.acha-ncha.org). Click on the ACHA-NCHA Data button. In the most recent executive summary, review the data tables of recent findings related to college students' health.
4. Review specifically the findings for violence, abusive relationships, and personal safety. Insert the data findings into **Table 1.3.2-1**.

Table 1.3.2-1 Violence, Abusive Relationships, and Personal Safety Data

Within the Last 12 Months, College Students Reported Experiencing:	Male %	Female %	Total %
A physical fight			
A physical assault (not sexual assault)			
A verbal threat			
Sexual touching without their consent			
Sexual penetration attempt without their consent			
Sexual penetration without their consent			
Stalking			
An emotionally abusive intimate relationship			
A physically abusive intimate relationship			
A sexually abusive intimate relationship			

Reproduced from American College Health Association. (2011). *American College Health Association—National college health assessment II: Reference group executive summary.* Spring 2011. Baltimore, MD: American College Health Association.

5. Compare the secondary data found in **Step 4** to the primary data provided by the instructor. Include in the comparison the following:
   a. The total percentage (%) of males and females who reported experiencing the 10 different types of violence and abusive behavior
   b. The percentage (%) of male college students who reported experiencing the 10 different types of violence and abusive behavior
   c. The percentage (%) of female college students who reported experiencing the 10 different types of violence and abusive behavior
6. Write recommendations for College XYZ of priorities for services and educational programs based upon citing both primary and secondary data.

Reference

American College Health Association. (2011). *American College Health Association—National college health assessment II: Reference group executive summary. Spring 2011.* Baltimore, MD: American College Health Association.

1.3.3 Identify Data Collection Instruments and Methods

Title Types of Needs Assessment Methods

Objective The student will be able to identify the differences among needs assessment methods.

Directions

1. Research each of the needs assessment methods listed in **Table 1.3.3-1**.
2. Complete **Table 1.3.3-1** with the information requested concerning the general purpose, advantages, and challenges for each method. Use the sample as a guide.
3. Select one of the needs assessment methods from **Table 1.3.3-1** and search for an example of an actual program or situation in which the method was used. In the space following the needs assessment methods, provide the program name, a brief description of the program or situation, and a reference for the source. Some help is provided in the following sample.

Sample

The nominal group technique was used to obtain input from African American women concerning how job factors impacted weight and how daily life factors affected physical activity for the purpose of designing a worksite weight control program.

Reference

Zunker, C., Cox, T., Wingo, B., Knight, B., Jefferson, W., & Ard, J. (2008). Using formative research to develop a worksite health promotion program for African American women. *Women Health*, *2*(48), 189–207.

Table 1.3.3-1 Differences of Needs Assessment Methods

Needs Assessment Methods	Purpose	Advantages	Challenges
Sample: Nominal group process	To achieve a consensus among a group and prioritize ideas	All group members participate. All ideas accepted.	Time consuming Participant bias
Focus group			
Key informant interview			
Community forum			
Delphi technique			
Surveys			
Observation			
Program name: **Need assessment used:** **Description of program with source:**			

1.3.4 Develop Data Collection Instruments and Methods

Title Development of a Pretest on Recycling

Objectives
1. The student will be able to develop a multiple choice pretest.
2. The student will be able to refine the pretest after receiving peer feedback.

Directions
1. Read the following *scenario*.
   A health educator has been assigned to be a guest speaker on recycling to a high school health class. The teacher is willing to administer the pretest and provide the results in advance so the health educator can focus on the presentation.
2. Develop a six-question, multiple choice pretest and include the following information:
   a. Title of pretest
   b. Directions for completing the pretest
   c. Six multiple choice questions covering important concepts on recycling
3. Bring five copies of the pretest to class on the assigned date. In small groups of five or six students, compare pretests within the group and provide feedback on each student's pretest as to clarity of directions and questions.
4. Incorporate suggestions from the peer critiques.

1.3.5 Train Personnel and Stakeholders Regarding Data Collection

Title Ensuring Quality in Data Collection Through Training

Objectives
1. The student will be able to identify the challenges to quality data collection.
2. The student will be able to formulate a training plan regarding quality data collection.

Directions

Part 1

1. An important challenge in data collection is to ensure that data are accurate, complete, and meet program requirements. Using standardized data collection procedures and frequent oversight of the data collection process can ensure quality of data. A health educator may be asked to train personnel and stakeholders regarding appropriate data collection methods. Lessons learned from practicing health educators may be very valuable to understanding how best to conduct such training. Contact a health educator who is responsible for conducting a needs assessment and/or collecting health-related data from constituents. Make arrangements for a brief interview (via telephone or person to person).

2. Use the interview form found in **Table 1.3.5-1** as a guide. Add two or three questions that are not on the form.

3. Send the interviewee a copy of the interview guide a few days before the interview.

4. Within 3 days after the interview, send a thank-you note to the interviewee.

Table 1.3.5-1 Interview Questions on Data Collection

Name of interviewee:
Job title:
Job responsibilities:
Interview questions   1. Describe the specific situation(s) in which you collect data or supervise the collection of data.   2. What method(s) of data collection do you use? Quantitative? Qualitative?   3. How would you define quality of data?

(continues)

Table 1.3.5-1 Interview Questions on Data Collection *(continued)*

4. What strategies do you or other program personnel use to ensure quality of data?

5. What are the most common barriers you experience in trying to obtain quality data?

6. What suggestions do you have to overcome the barriers to ensuring quality?

7. Do you train personnel or other stakeholders on data collection? If so, what content do you cover in the training? What training methods or formats do you think work best? Do you think the training is effective in ensuring the quality of data? Why or why not?

8. Other questions:

Part 2

1. Assume a health educator has been asked to train personnel and stakeholders regarding appropriate methods to ensure the quality of data collection when using focus groups, interviews, and electronic surveys.
2. Use **Table 1.3.5-2** as a guide to develop a detailed training plan. Consider using a combination of knowledge obtained from the interview in *Part 1*, previous coursework on data collection methods, and readings from the Community Tool Box at ctb.ku.edu/en/default .aspx, Chapters 3 and 12 (KU Work Group, 2010a, 2010b).

Student Resources

1. Consult with an instructor for a list of possible contacts for interviews.
2. University of Kansas, Work Group for Community Health and Development. (2011). *The community tool box.*
   http://ctb.ku.edu/en/default.aspx

Table 1.3.5-2 Training Plan for Ensuring Quality in Data Collection

Details of the plan
Target audience
Specific, Measurable, Achievable, Realistic, and Timely (SMART) learning objectives for the training
Content outline with time allocation
Training format and methods
Participant recruitment methods
Materials and resources needed
Training assessment methods

References

KU Work Group for Community Health and Development. (2010a). Assessing community needs and resources. In: *The community tool box* (Chapter 3). Lawrence: University of Kansas. Retrieved from http://ctb.ku.edu/en/tablecontents/chapter_1003.aspx

KU Work Group for Community Health and Development. (2010b). Providing training and technical assistance. In: *The community tool box* (Chapter 12). Lawrence: University of Kansas. Retrieved from http://ctb.ku.edu/en/tablecontents/chapter_1012.aspx

1.3.6 Use Data Collection Instruments and Methods

Title Community Profile

Objective The student will be able to utilize census data to identify demographic characteristics important for health education programming in a specific community.

Directions

1. Locate the most current government population census documents online by using the following Internet site: census.gov.
2. Select a community in your home state or the state in which you currently reside that has sufficient government data to respond to the community profile worksheet in **Table 1.3.6.1**.

Table 1.3.6-1 Community Profile

Profile of general demographic characteristics: Census year _____
Community profile of _____

Demographic Characteristics	Number	Percent
Total population		
Age		
Under 5 years		
5–9 years		
10–14 years		
15–19 years		
20–24 years		
25–34 years		
35–44 years		
45–54 years		
55–59 years		
60–64 years		
65–74 years		
75–84 years		
85 years and over		
Median Age		
Race		
White		
Black or African American		
American Indian and Alaska Native		

Table 1.3.6-1 Community Profile *(continued)*

Asian		
Native Hawaiian and Other Pacific Islander		
Hispanic or Latino (of any race)		
Household by type		
Average household size		
Average family size		
Female household, no husband present		
Educational attainment		
Less than 9th grade		
9th–12th grade, no diploma		
High school graduate (includes equivalency)		
Percent high school graduate or higher		
Percent bachelor's degree or higher		
Place of birth		
Native		
Foreign born		
Language spoken at home		
English only		
Language other than English		
Employment status—16 years and older		
In labor force		
Females 16 and over in labor force		
All parents in family in labor force with children under 6 years old		
Commuting to work		
Car, truck, or van—drove alone		
Car, truck, or van—car pooled		
Public transportation		
Walk		
Mean travel time to work (minutes)		
Income—most recent in dollars _____ (year)		

(continues)

Table 1.3.6-1 Community Profile *(continued)*

Demographic Characteristics	Number	Percent
Median household income		
Median family income		
Poverty status in _____ (year)		
Families		
Families with female householder, no husband		
Individuals		

Modified from U.S. Census Bureau. (2010). *Population finder.* Retrieved from http://www.census.gov.

Table 1.3.6-2 Importance of Selected Demographic Characteristics for Planning

Demographic Characteristics	Justify Importance for Health Education Planning in Selected Community
1.	
2.	
3.	

3. Complete the community profile worksheet by finding the *demographic profile* for the community selected by entering the statistical data in the spaces provided in **Table 1.3.6-1**.
4. Review the completed community profile information and select 3 of the 10 demographic characteristics that are important in planning health education programming for the community selected.
5. Identify in **Table 1.3.6-2** names of the three selected demographic characteristics and provide reasons why each characteristic is important for health education planning in the community selected.

Reference

U.S. Census Bureau. (2010). *Population finder.* Retrieved from http://www.census.gov

1.3.7 Employ Ethical Standards When Collecting Data

Title Applying Ethical Principles to Data Collection for Needs Assessment

Objectives
1. The student will be able to identify principles of ethical data collection to determine if data collection requires a review from an institutional review board.
2. The student will be able to demonstrate the principles of ethical data collection by developing a letter of informed consent to be used in data collection for needs assessment.

Directions

Part 1
1. Access the Washington State Department of Health at doh.wa.gov.
2. Read the document titled, "Human Subjects and Public Health Practice Guidelines for Ethical Data Collection."
3. The National Commission for Protection of Human Subjects (NIH, 1979) developed a framework that includes three ethical principles that should guide human research. The principles

Table 1.3.7-1 Questions to Guide Ethical Data Collection

Area of Data Collection	Question(s) to Consider	Indicate the Principles that the Area of Data Collection Addresses: Respect for Persons (R), Beneficence (B), and/or Justice (J). Highlight All That Apply.
Purpose		R B J
Methods		R B J
Risk and benefits		R B J
Confidentiality		R B J
Informed consent		R B J

are: (1) respect for persons, (2) beneficence, and (3) justice. To assure that data collection meets these ethical principles, a health educator should carefully consider the purpose, methods, population group, risk and benefits, confidentiality, and the informed consent process. In **Column 2** of **Table 1.3.7-1**, make a list of questions to ask when developing the plan for data collection according to each of these areas and in **Column 3** indicate if these questions address the ethical principle of respect for persons (R), beneficence (B), and/or justice (J).

Part 2

1. An institutional review board (IRB) is charged with reviewing data collection plans to assure compliance with the principles covered in *Part 1*. To learn more about this process, locate the institutional review board web page of a college/university or a healthcare/public health agency (governmental or private) to review the application procedures, specifically the criteria for exempt, expedited, and full institutional review. If no web page exists, contact the agency directly and request application materials.

2. Select at least two of the following needs assessment *scenarios*. In **Table 1.3.7-2**, list specific situations in which the data collection would be considered exempt or would require expedited or full review.

Scenario 1

A client satisfaction survey

Scenario 2

Interviewing community members to determine main health concerns

Scenario 3

Reviewing medical records to determine prevalence of a specific health condition

Scenario 4

Pencil-and-paper survey of middle school students to determine prevalence of risk behaviors

Scenario 5

Focus group to test a health promotion message

3. IRB applications require samples of letters of informed consent. Develop a letter of informed consent for one of the needs assessment *scenarios* from *Part 2*, **Step 2**. Make sure the letter includes the ethical principles presented in *Part 1* and is written in a way that is understood by the participants.

Table 1.3.7-2 Description of IRB Review Categories

Scenario	Exempt If...	Expedited Review If...	Full Review If...
1.			
2.			

Student Resources

1. National Institutes of Health, Office of Human Subjects Research. (1979). *The Belmont report: Ethical principles and guidelines for protection of human subjects of research.* Washington, DC: DHHS.
http://ohsr.od.nih.gov
In the search box, type "Belmont Report."
2. Washington State Department of Health (2008, December 11). *Human subjects and public health practice: Guidelines for ethical data collection.*
http://www.doh.wa.gov
In the search box, type "human subjects."

COMPETENCY 1.4 EXAMINE RELATIONSHIPS AMONG BEHAVIORAL, ENVIRONMENTAL, AND GENETIC FACTORS THAT ENHANCE OR COMPROMISE HEALTH

1.4.1 Identify Factors that Influence Health Behaviors

1.4.2 Analyze Factors that Influence Health Behaviors

Title Health Determinants Investigation and Analysis

Objectives

1. The student will be able to identify factors influencing health behaviors within categories and type of impact upon health behavior.
2. The student will be able to describe how physical, social, emotional, intellectual, and environmental factors influence health behaviors.

Directions

1. List in **Table 1.4.1-1** specific factors that foster or hinder health behaviors in each of the following categories: physical, social, emotional, intellectual, and environmental. One example of a social factor that hinders health behavior is poverty.
2. In small groups, analyze in depth how one hindering and one fostering factor specifically influences a category of health behavior, as assigned by the instructor.
3. As a group, summarize the group analysis in **Step 2** to share in class.

Table 1.4.1-1 Specific Factors that Hinder or Foster Health Behaviors

Categories of Factors	Specific Factors that Hinder and Foster Health Behavior
Physical	
Hinder	1. 2.
Foster	1. 2.
Social	
Hinder	1. 2.
Foster	1. 2.

Table 1.4.1-1 Specific Factors that Hinder or Foster Health Behaviors *(continued)*

Emotional	
Hinder	1. 2.
Foster	1. 2.

Intellectual	
Hinder	1. 2.
Foster	1. 2.

Environmental	
Hinder	1. 2.
Foster	1. 2.

1.4.3 Identify Factors that Enhance or Compromise Health

1.4.4 Analyze Factors that Enhance or Compromise Health

Title Lifestyle Influences on Health

Objectives
1. The student will be able to identify behaviors that enhance or compromise health.
2. The student will be able to analyze behaviors that enhance or compromise health.

Directions
1. List five behaviors that tend to enhance and five behaviors that tend to compromise health. Record the specific behaviors in the appropriate column in **Table 1.4.3-1**.
2. For each health-enhancing behavior, describe how the behavior positively affects health. Similarly, describe how each health-compromising behavior negatively affects health. Provide examples of how the behavior contributes to specific disorders and/or diseases. Record the responses in the appropriate columns in **Table 1.4.3-1**.

Table 1.4.3-1 Behaviors Enhancing or Compromising Health Status

Specific Behavior Description	Enhancing +	Explanation of Positive Effects upon Health
1.		
2.		
3.		
4.		
5.		
Specific Behavior Description	**Compromising –**	**Explanation of Negative Effects upon Health**
1.		
2.		
3.		
4.		
5.		

COMPETENCY 1.5 EXAMINE FACTORS THAT INFLUENCE THE LEARNING PROCESS

1.5.1 Identify Factors that Foster or Hinder the Learning Process

Title The Learning Process: Identifying Factors that Influence It

Objective The student will be able to identify positive and negative effects upon learning process of various age groups.

Directions

1. Use ERIC to find the type and amount of literature on factors that affect the learning process of one of the three age groups.
   a. Children
   b. Adolescents
   c. Adults
2. Complete **Table 1.5.1-1** by listing three factors that hinder, impede, delay, or slow the learning process and three factors that foster, support, or promote the learning process for the selected age group.
3. Provide definitions, examples, or research data for each of the listed factors that support why it is a hindering or fostering effect upon student learning.
4. For each factor, provide an in-text citation in the table and create a reference list. Use the reference style identified by the instructor to record the list in the space below the section on fostering factors.
5. Write in the space provided how this table of information will be useful to the health educator conducting a needs assessment.

Table 1.5.1-1 Factors Influencing Learning Process of Selected Age Group

Age Group	Factors Fostering or Hindering the Learning Process
Sample: Adults	**Hindering factors**
	Sample: Lifetime acquired knowledge may make it difficult to learn new things that are in conflict (Kerner & Weinerman, 2011).
	1.
	2.
	3.

(continues)

Table 1.5.1-1 Factors Influencing Learning Process of Selected Age Group *(continued)*

	Fostering factors
	1.
	2.
	3.

Sample reference
Kenner, C., & Weinerman, J. (2011). Adult learning theory: Applications to non-traditional college students. *Journal of College Reading and Learning, 41*(2), 87–96.

Usefulness of Table 1.5.1-1 for the health education assessment process

1.5.3 Identify Factors that Foster or Hinder Attitudes and Beliefs

1.5.4 Analyze Factors that Foster or Hinder Attitudes and Beliefs

Title Tobacco Prevention Needs Assessment

Objectives

1. The student will be able to identify factors that influence beliefs and attitudes of adolescents toward tobacco use.
2. The student will be able to cite research data on attitudes and beliefs factors influencing adolescents toward use or nonuse of tobacco use.

Directions

1. Completing **Activity 1.5.1** first will help with this activity.
2. Read the following *scenario*.

   Recently, a group of concerned individuals from a variety of organizations in your community got together to discuss how to prevent adolescent tobacco use in the county. Their intent is to form a coalition that eventually will plan, implement, and evaluate a tobacco use reduction program. A group member has made contact with a health educator seeking background data and information about factors that influence the beliefs and attitudes of adolescents toward tobacco use.

3. Identify three factors in **Table 1.5.3-1** that hinder and also three factors that foster adolescents' beliefs or attitudes related to tobacco use. For each of the listed factors, provide definitions, examples, and research data that support why it is a hindering or fostering effect. Reference sources and provide in-text citations for each factor identified in the table. Review **Student Resources** for help.
4. Select and highlight in blue three factors from either or both rows that are most important to share with the group of concerned individuals.
5. Explain why each factor has been chosen as one of the three most important factors.

Student Resources

1. Centers for Disease Control and Prevention
   Youth Tobacco Prevention
   http://www.cdc.gov
   In the search box, type "tobacco, youth."

Table 1.5.3-1 Factors Influencing Adolescent Attitudes or Beliefs Toward Tobacco Use

Types of Influence Upon Adolescent Attitudes or Beliefs	Influencing Factors Specific to Tobacco Use Supported by Research Data
Hindering factors	
Fostering factors	

2. Tobacco-Free Maine
   http://www.tobaccofreemaine.org
3. Healthy People 2010: Understanding and Improving Health
   http://www.healthypeople.gov
   Find the "Tobacco Objectives."
4. Audrain-McGovern, J., Rodriguez, D., Patel, V., Faith, M. S., Rodgers, K., & Cuevas, J. (2006). How do psychological factors influence adolescent smoking progression? The evidence for indirect effects through tobacco advertising receptivity. *Pediatrics, 117*, 1216–1225. doi:10.1542/peds.2005-0808

   http://www.pediatrics.aapublications.org

   a. Navigate to the eArchives.
   b. Select 2006. Select April.
   c. Find the article by scrolling down to the correct page numbers.

COMPETENCY 1.6 EXAMINE FACTORS THAT ENHANCE OR COMPROMISE THE PROCESS OF HEALTH EDUCATION

1.6.1 Determine the Extent of Available Health Education Programs, Interventions, and Policies

Title Community Health Status Indicators Data of Selected Counties

Objective The student will be able to identify the availability and utilization of preventive health services in a selected target county and one peer county.

Directions

1. Open the Community Health Status Indicators (CHSI) web page.
2. From the drop lists at the CHSI website, select a state and county. The county will be identified as the target county for this activity. Enter the selected state and county in **Table 1.6.1-1** below the *sample*.
3. Click on the Display Data button.
4. Scroll down to the Peer County List to select a peer county that can be compared to the selected target county. If the selected target county has no peer county identified or has too little data, choose another target county in a nearby state. Enter the name of the selected peer county and state and in the appropriate spaces in **Table 1.6.1-1**.
5. Click on the Preventive Services Use link. Next, enter data on Adult Preventive Services Use (%) for the peer county.

Table 1.6.1-1 Comparison of Utilization Percentages of Selected Adult Preventive Services by State and County

State and County	Pap Smears	Mammography	Sigmoidoscopy	Pneumonia	Flu Vaccines
Sample Target County: Cambria County, PA	74.6%	68.5%	36%	60.3%	73.6%
Sample Peer County: Lackawanna County, PA	77.3%	77.2%	47.0%	59.3%	65.0%
Target:					
Peer:					
Findings					

6. Return to the target county to complete needed utilization information in **Table 1.6.1-1**.
7. In the bottom row of **Table 1.6.1-1**, record the findings of the most significant differences between the selected target county and peer county (not the samples). Project reasons why these differences may have occurred.

Student Resource

Community Health Status Indicators (CHSI) web page
http://www.communityhealth.hhs.gov

Reference

Department of Health and Human Services. (2009). *Community health status indicators*. (2009). Retrieved from http://www.communityhealth.hhs.gov/HomePage.aspx

1.6.2 Assess the Quality of Available Health Education Programs, Interventions, and Policies

Title Just How Good Is This Drug Abuse Prevention Program?

Objective The student will be able to assess the quality of health education programs or interventions.

Directions

1. The Substance Abuse and Mental Health Services Administration (SAMHSA) is a part of the U.S. Department of Health and Human Services (DHHS, 2011). It houses a national registry of evidence-based programs and practices (NREPP). Open SAMHSA's national registry of evidence-based programs and practices at nrepp.samhsa.gov. This site is a searchable online registry of interventions in mental health promotion, substance abuse prevention, and other topics.

2. In the search box, use a key word to search for a substance abuse prevention program of interest. Click on the Search button. Click on the link for a program of interest to review.

3. Choose one program to assess and record responses to the following questions.
    a. What is the name of the program, and what is its intention (prevention, intervention, or treatment)?
    b. The program has been designed to achieve what outcomes?
    c. Describe the target population with specifics on age, gender, ethnicity, settings, and others.

4. Scroll down and find the link titled, "Quality of Research." Click on the link and review at least two research articles about the chosen drug abuse prevention program.

5. Answer the following questions from only one of the research articles read.
    a. Does the program produce the desired changes in the population it is targeting?
    b. Was the research conducted by reputable researchers and published in a reputable journal?
    c. Did the study use a rigorous evaluation design?
    d. What were the negative effects of the program listed in the study?
    e. Was the study replicated at more than one site?
    f. Was the program implemented by those who would eventually administer it in their agency (for example, if it was to be implemented in a school, did school staff implement it in the study)?

6. Record a summary of the article reviewed that includes assessment of the quality and outcome of the program with justification followed by a recommendation for use of this program.

Reference

U. S. Department of Health and Human Services, Substance Abuse and Mental Health Services. (2011, January). *National registry of evidence-based programs and practices*. Retrieved from http://nrepp.samhsa.gov

1.6.3 Identify Existing and Potential Partners for the Provision of Health Education

Title Identifying Stakeholders for Health Promotion

Objective The student will be able to identify key stakeholders in the community with a vested interest in health promotion.

Directions

1. Select a health promotion issue and/or a specific health promotion program of personal interest and select a target community.
2. Use **Table 1.6.3-1** to identify key stakeholders in the community that have a vested interest in the health issue and/or health promotion program. List the names of specific stakeholders, where possible. See the list of **Student Resources** for sources of information to consult for making the list.

Student Resources

1. Yellow pages
2. Town directories
3. Chamber of commerce
4. Newspapers
5. Websites
6. Friends
7. Colleagues

Table 1.6.3-1 Key Stakeholders for a Specific Health Promotion Issue/Program

Health promotion issue/program:

Target audience:

Key Stakeholder Category	Name(s) of Stakeholder(s)
Businesses	
Civic groups	
Concerned citizens	
Faith-based organizations	
Health services	
Justice and law enforcement agencies	
Local government	
Media	
Nongovernmental organizations	
Nonprofit organizations	
Schools/universities	
Target population	
Volunteer advocacy organizations	
Other	

1.6.4 Assess Social, Environmental, and Political Conditions that May Impact Health Education

Title Assessing Factors that Impede Health Promotion Activities

Objective The student will be able to conduct an assessment of the social, environmental, and/or political factors that impede health promotion activities.

Directions

1. Read the following *scenarios.*

Scenario 1

Nearly 10 years ago, with a goal of providing citizens physical activity opportunities, a city had invested several million dollars in building a recreational complex complete with tennis courts, soccer, baseball, football fields, basketball courts, a golf course, playgrounds, several miles of walking/running trails, and a water park/swimming pool. Recently, a group of concerned citizens addressed the city commission stating that a subpopulation within the city was not accessing the facilities due to lack of safe sidewalks and/or crosswalks and lack of public transportation to and from the facilities. The city recently has experienced a severe economic crisis that included a multimillion-dollar loss in the city's investments and increased unemployment due to the closing of a factory that employed nearly 1,000 people. While the city officials are sensitive to the disparities in access to the facilities, they are not in favor of taking any immediate action.

Scenario 2

A small, rural county has a teen pregnancy rate that is 10% higher than the state rate and nearly 15% higher than the national rate. A teen pregnancy prevention coalition has been in place for several years but struggles to gain access to the target population and to persons/institutions of influence to teens. As a result, it hired an external contractor to conduct key informant interviews and focus groups. Social stigma of teen pregnancy (parents and teens being ashamed), belief in an abstinence-only approach as the best method, denial among key stakeholders that teen pregnancy should be addressed, and lack of political will to provide resources for teen pregnancy prevention were cited as reasons for lack of participation in teen pregnancy prevention initiatives.

2. For each *scenario*, list factors that might impede an individual's willingness to participate in a program, ability to internalize health information, and/or ability to participate in a prevention program. Label each factor as social, environmental, and/or political. Record responses in appropriate sections in **Table 1.6.4-1**.

Table 1.6.4-1 Assessment of Social, Environmental, and Political Factors Impeding Health Promotion

Scenario 1: Factors That Impede Health Education	Is the Factor Social (S), Environmental (E), and/or Political (P)? Highlight All That Apply.	Scenario 2: Factors That Impede Health Education	Is the Factor Social (S), Environmental (E), and/or Political (P)? Highlight All That Apply.
	S E P		S E P
	S E P		S E P
	S E P		S E P
	S E P		S E P

3. Provide a response to the following questions:
   a. Are the factors identified in the *scenarios* within the control of the health educator? Justify the response.
   b. Given these conditions, describe the impact and/or challenges that each of these present for the health educator.

1.6.5 Analyze the Capacity for Developing Needed Health Education

Title Mapping Community Capacity: Who, What, and Where Are the Assets?

Objective The student will be able to analyze assets to determine capacity for health promotion.

Directions

1. Assume that a coalition on a college or university campus has a goal of increasing physical activity of students, staff, and faculty and is interested in conducting an assets-based, or capacity, assessment. Complete the asset-based (capacity) inventory as outlined in **Table 1.6.5-1** for the selected campus. Identify the existing assets for promoting physical activity of the campus/community.
2. Obtain a map of a college/university. Using the assets identified in **Step 1**, map assets related to physical activity by matching the asset with the location on campus.
3. Analyze the map of the assets by answering the following questions:
   a. Where are the assets located?
   b. Are assests dispersed or are they concentrated in a certain area?
   c. What results were found that were expected?
   d. What results were found that were unexpected?
   e. What recommendations could be made to the coalition based on the asset-based assessment and map? Why?

Student Resources

1. Map of the campus and/or nearby community for the mapping activity (consider enlarging the map)
2. Color pencils and/or markers, small sticky notes for adding notation to the map

Table 1.6.5-1 Asset-Based Inventory

Selected campus:	
Types of Assets	**Identified Assets**
Individual assets (e.g., skills, abilities, communication networks, income)	
Clubs/special interest groups (e.g., faith-based, student, cultural)	
Agencies/organizations (e.g., police departments, parks, libraries, non-profit organizations, hospitals/health centers)	
Physical resources (e.g., facilities, green space, buildings, sidewalks, streets, energy, land)	

1.6.6 Assess the Need for Resources to Foster Health Education

Title Formal and Informal Resource Assessment

Objective The student will be able to identify financial and human resource needs for health promotion programs using formal and informal assessment methods.

Directions

Part 1

1. Use a sample logic model of a health promotion program provided by the instructor to determine the financial and human resources needed to support the program. Complete **Table 1.6.6-1** by listing the specific resources needed in each category (financial and human resources) and by providing a brief justification for the resource need (i.e., what activity/ output or outcome is fulfilled with the resource).
2. Identify a local health promotion program. Make arrangements for a brief interview (via telephone or person to person) with the program administrator to discuss resource needs for the program.
3. Use the interview guide found in **Table 1.6.6-2**. Add two to three questions to the list.
4. Send the interviewee a copy of the interview guide a few days before the interview.
5. Conduct the interview.
6. Send a thank you note to the interviewee within 3 days after the interview.
7. Write at the bottom of **Table 1.6.6-2** a narrative describing the greatest resource needs and/ or gaps of the program based on the findings from the interview.

Part 2

Compare and contrast methods of assessing resource needs by identifying advantages and disadvantages of the two methods in this activity. Record responses in **Table 1.6.6-3**.

Student Resources

1. Sample logic model for a health promotion program provided by instructor
2. List of local and/or regional health promotion programs along with contact information provided by instructor

Reference

KU Work Group for Community Health and Development. (2011). Identifying community assets and resources. In: *The community tool box* (Chapter 3, Section 8). Lawrence: University of Kansas. Retrieved from http://ctb.ku.edu/en/tablecontents/section_1043.aspx

Table 1.6.6-1 Financial and Human Resource Needs for a Health Promotion Program

Financial Resources Needed	Justification
Human Resources Needed	Justification

Table 1.6.6-2 Program Resource Needs Interview Guide

Interviewee information

Name:

Agency/organization name:

Job title:

Address:

Phone number:

Interview questions

1. What kinds of services does your organization provide to the community? What kinds of projects is your organization involved in now?

2. What groups or subpopulations does your organization/program target?

3. How many people are part of your organization/program?

   Staff?

   Volunteers?

   Other contributors?

   Board members?

4. How many clients do you serve?

5. What are the sources of funding for your organization/program?

6. What categories are included in your program budget?

7. Are there services not being offered because of insufficient funding?

8. What physical spaces does your organization have access to for both program implementation and administration?

9. What kind of equipment does your organization have access to?

   Office?

   Audiovisual or video?

   Computers?

   Mechanical?

   Other?

10. What kind of written media materials/newsletters does your organization have?

11. What other organizations do you work with? What other organizations does your group sponsor events with? Share information with? Share resources or equipment with?

12. Who else does work for or provides similar services to the community as those provided by your organization?

13. From your perspective, are there gaps in services provided to the target population?

Other questions:

(continues)

Table 1.6.6-2 Program Resource Needs Interview Guide *(continued)*

Summary paragraph

Adapted from KU Work Group for Community Health and Development. (2011). Identifying community assets and resources: Chapter 3, Section 8. Lawrence, KS: University of Kansas. Retrieved from http://ctb.ku.edu

Table 1.6.6-3 Advantages and Disadvantages of Method Types to Assess Resource Needs

Method Name	Advantages	Disadvantages
	1. 2. 3.	1. 2. 3.
	1. 2. 3.	1. 2. 3.

COMPETENCY 1.7 INFER NEEDS FOR HEALTH EDUCATION BASED ON ASSESSMENT FINDINGS

1.7.1 Analyze Assessment Findings

Title Analysis of Community Health Status Indicators Data Findings of Selected Counties

Objective The student will be able to analyze the availability and utilization patterns of preventive health services in a target county and compare findings to a peer county.

Directions

1. Review completed **Activity 1.6.1 Community Health Status Indicators Data of Selected Counties** findings recorded for a selected target county and appropriate peer county.
2. Analyze and summarize the findings in **Table 1.6.1-1** by writing a paragraph for each of the following areas in the space provided in **Table 1.7.1-1**.
   a. Compare similarities and differences of data findings on adult preventive services use for the selected target and its peer county. In what areas is the target county better than, or and worse than, the peer county?
   b. Analyze only the target county data findings. What are possible reasons for low or high percentages of adult preventive services use in that county?
   c. Suggest two ways of adult preventive services that could be increased for the target county.

Student Resource

Community Health Status Indicators (CHSI) web page
http://www.communityhealth.hhs.gov

Table 1.7.1-1 Summary of Analysis and Conclusions

Target county:	Peer county:
Target county state:	Peer county state:
Target and peer county similarities and differences:	
Target county analysis:	
Ways to increase adult preventive services use in target county:	

1.7.3 Prioritize Health Education Needs

1.7.4 Identify Emerging Health Education Needs

1.7.5 Report Assessment Findings

Title Prioritize and Report Health Education Needs

Objectives
1. The student will be able to apply a step-by-step model to prioritize health needs.
2. The student will be able to identify emerging health education needs.
3. The student will be able to share assessment findings through presentation software.

Directions
1. For this activity, read the background information provided and review the information about prioritizing community health issues in **Student Resources**.

Background Information
After reviewing the available data collected through a community diagnosis, a local county community health council compiled and defined key health issues for its community. Following is a list of the most concerning issues for the community along with the corresponding data available for each issue as most recently reported.
   a. Poverty: 23% of county residents are listed as impoverished.
   b. Poor or fair health: 15% of residents have self-reported health status as poor.
   c. Access to healthy food: 31% of the zip codes in the county have healthy food outlets.
   d. Adult obesity: 39% of adults in the county are classified as obese.
   e. Unemployment: 9% of county residents are unemployed.
2. After a careful review of the data, use **Table 1.7.3-1** to rank the five health issues starting with the most concerning issue to the least based on justified reasons.

Table 1.7.3-1 Top Five Most Concerning Health Issues

Highest Concern to Lowest Concern	Health Issue
1.	
2.	
3.	
4.	
5.	
Reasons for ranking	

50

3. Check **Student Resources** to begin an Internet search for the following questions:
   a. Which issues are expected to increase in incidence/prevalence in the future?
   b. What are some of the predicted future trends for each of the issues?
   c. How does each issue impact overall health status?
   d. What is the feasibility of implementing effective interventions for each issue as supported by data in professional journal articles?
4. Record in **Table 1.7.4-1** the Internet search findings for the first three concerning issues listed in **Table 1.7.3-1** for each of the following three categories.
   a. Proportion of the population impacted (prevalence/incidence)
   b. Seriousness of the issue (severity of consequences)
   c. Likelihood the issue can be successfully impacted through available evidence-based interventions
5. Based on **Steps 2** and **3**, complete **Table 1.7.5-1** by rank, ordering the three most concerning health issues again. Identify reasons supported by studies and research with references for any changes in the rank order.
6. Develop a visual presentation of 5 to 10 slides using PowerPoint or a similar software program. The presentation should include prioritization of the first and second rankings of the

Table 1.7.4-1 Internet Findings by Category and Most Concerning Issues

Impact incidence/prevalence
Issue 1
Issue 2
Issue 3
Seriousness of issue
Issue 1
Issue 2
Issue 3
Feasibility of evidence-based interventions
Issue 1
Issue 2
Issue 3

Table 1.7.5-1 Priority of Health Issues Needing Interventions Based on Research Findings

Highest Concern to Lowest Concern	Health Issue	Reasons for Ranking Order with References
1.		
2.		
3.		

3 most concerning health issues, reasons for original ranking and second ranking, key assessment findings relevant to the background information in **Step 1**, and potential evidence-based interventions for health needs.

7. Share work with two classmates by exchanging hard copies or an electronic version of the presentation.

Student Resources

1. Association of State and Territorial Dental Directors
   http.www.astdd.org
   In the search box, type "assessing oral health needs."
2. U.S. Census Bureau. Poverty
   http://www.census.gov
   In the search box, type "poverty."
3. Access to Healthy Foods Coalition web page
   http://www.accesstohealthyfoods.org
4. Centers for Disease Control and Prevention
   http://www.cdc.gov
   Type "health-related quality of life" or "HRQOL" in the search box.
5. Centers for Disease Control and Prevention
   http://www.cdc.gov
   Type "overweight and obesity" or "obesity trends" in the search box.
6. United States Bureau of Labor. Overview of Bureau of Labor Statistics on Unemployment
   http://www.bls.gov
   In the search box, type "unemployment."

Plan Health Education

INTRODUCTION

After the assessment of needs is completed, the planning process begins. Included in this chapter are 21 activities that address 21 entry-level sub-competencies in Area of Responsibility II.

Activities in this chapter provide experiences for the student in examining the role of stakeholders and priority populations in planning and for creating goal and outcome statements. A series of scenarios provide opportunities for the students to practice identifying, recruiting, and obtaining commitments from stakeholders to help with a community program. Additional scenarios will challenge students to identify potential resources needed for programs as well as analyze factors that contribute to or hinder successful program planning.

The role of theory for developing interventions and strategies is introduced. Students will apply principles of cultural competence to create, select, and evaluate interventions for use in programs for diverse populations. Activities will require them to practice the skills of pilot testing and applying the *Code of Ethics for the Health Education Profession* in the design of interventions and strategies.

Students also will begin to gain practical experiences on how to organize strategies and interventions in a logical scope and sequence to fit the needs of a program. Two activities require students to apply the Centers for Disease Control and Prevention's Health Education Curriculum Analysis Tool (HECAT) and the Community Health Assessment aNd Group Evaluation (CHANGE) tool to an actual school health program for the purpose of designing content for a workshop and integrating health education into existing programs.

Some topics addressed in this chapter include weight management, college health concerns, work site tobacco policies, and HIV/AIDS.

For this text, please go to the student companion website at **go.jblearning.com/PracticalApp** to complete activities using e-templates, and then pass your completed activities to your instructor for review of grading.

COMPETENCY 2.1 INVOLVE PRIORITY POPULATIONS AND OTHER STAKEHOLDERS IN THE PLANNING PROCESS

2.1.1 Incorporate Principles of Community Organization

Title Principles of Community Organization in Planning Process

Objective The student will be able to describe the principles of community organization for use in future coalition-building efforts.

Directions

1. Read the material about principles (also called processes or steps) of community organization provided by the course instructor.
2. Define/discuss the following terms: *community organization, stakeholder, community capacity, community and capacity building, social capital, coalition, priority population, grassroots participation*, and *empowered community*. These terms are important to an understanding of the principles involved in this sub-competency.
3. Use **Table 2.1.1-1** to describe the principles (referred to as steps by McKenzie, Pinger, & Kotecki, 2012) in community organization.
4. Read the following *scenario.*
   A major city has a large population with type 2 diabetes. A health educator in an outpatient medical setting recognizes the need for a diabetes self-management education program in the

Table 2.1.1-1 Principles (Steps) in Community Organization

Principles (Steps)	Description of Principle (Step)
1. Recognizing the issue	
2. Gaining entry into the community	
3. Organizing the people	
4. Assessing the community	
5. Determining the priorities and setting goals	
6. Arriving at a solution and selecting intervention strategies	
7. Implementing the plan	
8. Evaluating the outcomes of the plan of action	
9. Maintaining the outcomes in the community	
10. Looping back	

Modified from McKenzie, J. F., Pinger, R. R., & Kotecki, J. E. (2012). *An introduction to community health* (7th ed., pp. 125–131). Burlington, MA: Jones & Bartlett Learning.

community being served. Gaining entry into the community involves contacting stakeholders and priority populations. Phone book yellow and white pages can be found at switchboard.com.

5. Choose a larger city that interests you. Using a phone book, locate the address and phone number of one or two organizations that fit each of the categories listed in **Table 2.1.1-2**. When locating organizations/agencies, think about how they can be useful in the development of a diabetes self-management education program.

Student Resources

1. The Community Tool Box has information on community organizing efforts in Chapter 1, Section 8.
http://ctb.ku.edu

2. The Community Guide is a resource to assist health educators to review and select health promotion and disease prevention programs.
http://thecommunityguide.org

3. Alcohol Justice has information on community organization and examples of community organization efforts
http://www.alcoholjustice.org

Reference

McKenzie, J. F., Pinger, R. R., & Kotecki, J. E. (2012). *An introduction to community health* (7th ed., pp. 125–131). Burlington, MA: Jones & Bartlett Learning.

Table 2.1.1-2 Organizations to Call Seeking Support

City or town selected_____		
Types of Community Organizations	**Organization/Agency Name**	**Organization/Agency Address and Phone Number**
1. Parks and recreation		
2. Grassroots		
3. Healthcare providers		
4. Human/social services		
5. Education		
6. Government		
7. Faith community		
8. Law enforcement		
9. Neighborhood associations		
10. Civic volunteers		
11. Businesses		
12. Media		
13. Other		

2.1.2 Identify Priority Populations and Other Stakeholders

Title Community Involvement: A Case Scenario

Objective The student will be able to identify key stakeholders needed to plan a program in the community.

Directions

1. Read the *scenario.*

   A health educator is working at a health department in a community of 50,000 people. A needs assessment has identified a high level of skin cancer as the top priority of this community. The health educator wants to develop a health education program to reduce the risk of skin cancer. This community has a hospital as well as other community agencies. The hospital and other resource people have been identified and contacted, but have expressed little interest in becoming involved. All agree that it is a worthy and needed program, but few see how their input would be beneficial to the program or to themselves.

2. Discuss the definition of priority populations and the definition of stakeholders.

3. Using **Table 2.1.2-1**, determine the potential community organizations and resource people who might have interest in being involved in a community's effort to provide this program. Think about the types of motivations, priorities, and goals of various key agencies/organizations and how one can express need for the skin cancer prevention program in ways that relate to their community jobs or roles.

Table 2.1.2-1 Identifying Priority Populations and Potential Stakeholders

Potential Community Stakeholders and Justified Priority Populations	Explain Why Each Stakeholder Should Be Considered and Provide Justification for Priority Populations or Targeted Audiences
Potential health-related agencies to be involved: For example, American Cancer Society List others:	
Other potential stakeholders in the community:	
Priority populations—those most at risk for skin cancer:	

2.1.3 Communicate Need for Health Education to Priority Populations and Other Stakeholders

Title Communicating the Need: A Case Scenario

Objective The student will be able to identify several methods of communicating the need for the development of a program.

Directions

In **Activity 2.1.2**, a list of stakeholders and priority populations was developed for the following *case scenario*.

A health educator works at a health department in a community of 50,000 people. Findings of a recent needs assessment have revealed a high level of skin cancer as the top priority for this community. The local health department health educator wants to develop a health education program to reduce the risk of skin cancer.

Using **Table 2.1.3-1**, list several methods of communicating the need for a skin cancer risk reduction program in this community.

Table 2.1.3-1 Communicating Need for a Skin Cancer Risk Reduction Program

Method of Communication	Description of Method, Target Audience, and Focus of Message
1.	
2.	
3.	
4.	
5.	

2.1.4 Develop Collaborative Efforts Among Priority Populations and Other Stakeholders

Title Recruitment of Priority Populations and Stakeholders in Coalition Building

Objective The student will be able to describe a partner or coalition organization's mission and explain how to collaborate.

Directions

1. A checklist for creating and maintaining a coalition or partnership can be found in the Community Tool Box (ctb.ku.edu), Chapter 5, Sections 5 and 6 (KU Work Group, 2010a, 2010b). Form small groups to discuss this checklist, describing the steps necessary to create effective coalitions.
2. The county school system wants to develop a program to teach students the dangers of smoking and desires to partner with the American Cancer Society in developing a smoking prevention program for students. As the health educator, explain why this would be a beneficial collaboration. Record responses to this question and the remaining steps.
3. What is the mission of the American Cancer Society? Does the mission support partnership with the school system when developing this program? Why or why not?
4. Who else in the community might fit into this collaboration and why?
5. Who should be involved from the school system, besides the health educator?
6. Create three goals that the partnership could accomplish.

Student Resources

1. The Community Tool Box is a resource for community organizing efforts. Review Chapter 1, Section 8.
   http://ctb.ku.edu
2. The Community Guide is a resource to assist health educators in reviewing and selecting health promotion/disease prevention programs.
   http://thecommunityguide.org

References

KU Work Group for Community Health and Development. (2010a). Coalition building I: Starting a coalition. In: *The community tool box* (Chapter 5, Section 5). Lawrence: University of Kansas. Retrieved from http://ctb.ku.edu/en/tablecontents/sub_section_main_1057.aspx

KU Work Group for Community Health and Development. (2010b). Coalition building II: Maintaining a coalition. In: *The community tool box* (Chapter 5, Section 6). Lawrence: University of Kansas. Retrieved from http://ctb.ku.edu/en/tablecontents/section_1058.aspx

2.1.5 Elicit Input from Priority Populations and Other Stakeholders

Title Using a Focus Group

Objective The student will be able to elicit input from priority populations and other stakeholders using a focus group method.

Directions

1. Review some of the information on focus groups in **Student Resources**.
2. Read the following *scenario*.
   A health educator in a university setting has been asked by the student life advisory committee to plan a prevention program aimed at reducing the incidence of underage drinking by students. The health educator has chosen to use focus groups to determine what issues are most important to be addressed in the program.
3. Complete the information on planning for a focus group asked for in **Table 2.1.5-1**.

Table 2.1.5-1 Focus Group Development

Focus Group Development Topics	Respond to the Following Questions
Questions or interview guide	What questions would one ask that might provide insight and focus for this program direction?
Composition of focus group	Which individuals on or off campus might provide useful information about the issue or target group?
Recruiting	How will focus group participants be recruited?
Incentives	What kind of incentives could be offered to the participants for their time?
Setting	What location might be the best for the focus groups to meet?
Time allocation	How long should focus group sessions last?
Recording participant responses	How will participant responses be recorded?
Ground rules	After reviewing the recommendations in the literature, what are ground rules for the facilitator and participants to follow during the focus group process? Cite sources.
Reporting	How will the results of the focus groups be reported to the student life advisory committee and focus group participants?

Student Resources

1. The National Cancer Institute has an online resource called Making Health Communications Work: A Planner's Guide.
   http://www.cancer.gov
   In the search box, type "health communications."
2. A comparison is available of focus group versus individual interviews.
   http://cancercontrol.cancer.gov
   In the search box, type "focus groups."
3. Focus groups examples can be found at the Centers for Disease Control and Prevention website.
   http://www.cdc.gov
   Type "using focus groups" in the search box.
4. A guide to using focus groups in program development and evaluation can be found at University of Kentucky College of Agriculture.
   http://www.ca.uky.edu
   a. Click on the Extension link.
   b. Under Cooperative Extension Service (CES) Programs, click on Program & Staff Development.
   c. Click on the Program Development tab.
   d. Click on the Learn about Program Development tab on the right side of the screen.
   e. Publications and fact sheets about program development will be listed. Under Gathering Resident Perspectives, find information on focus groups.

2.1.6 Obtain Commitments from Priority Populations and Other Stakeholders

Title Recruiting for Operation Smoke Screen

Objective The student will be able to identify community members and agencies to contact to obtain their commitments to be involved in a smoking prevention program.

Directions

1. A health educator has been asked to develop a community prevention and intervention program aimed at smokers under age 18. Using **Table 2.1.6-1**, identify 10 individuals and/or agencies within the community (by job title or agency type) who are potential stakeholders in the development of the program.
2. Explain why the identified potential stakeholder should be involved in planning the program.
3. Review the proper format for writing a business letter in **Student Resources** before beginning this portion of the activity.
4. Compose a business letter adhering to the format in **Table 2.1.6-2** to send to individuals or agencies identified in **Table 2.1.6-1**.
5. Complete Intent of Commitment form by filling in types of support needed from the 10 stakeholders in **Table 2.1.6-3**. Enclose or attach this form with the letter created in **Step 4**.

Student Resources

1. The National Cancer Institute has an online resource called Making Health Communications Work. A Planner's Guide.
   http://www.cancer.gov
   Enter "Making health communications work" in the search box.
2. The following websites may be helpful when composing business letters.
   http://owl.english.purdue.edu
   http://writing.colostate.edu

Table 2.1.6-1 Stakeholder Recruitment for Operation Smoke Screen

List Agency or Individual Name, by Job Title or Agency Type	Why Should That Agency or Person Be Involved?
1.	
2.	
3.	
4.	
5.	
6.	
7.	
8.	
9.	
10.	

Table 2.1.6-2 Business Letter Format

Contact information (your contact information)

Name

Address

City, state, zip code

Phone number

Email address

Date

Contact information (the person or company to whom the letter is sent)

Name

Title

Company

Address

City, state, zip code

Salutation

Dear Mr./Ms./Mrs. Last Name:

Use a formal salutation, not a first name.

Body of the business letter

When writing a business letter, keep the letter simple and targeted so the purpose of your letter is clear. Single space the letter and leave a space between paragraphs. Left-justify the letter.

The first paragraph of your business letter should provide an introduction of yourself and an explanation of why you are writing the letter.

In a letter for this activity, the second paragraph should provide brief details about the plan for a community prevention and intervention program aimed at smokers under age 18.

For this activity, the following paragraph should seek the level of interest and support from the person to whom the letter is written. Explain types of ways one could support the program and the enclosed Intent of Commitment form with a return date for response.

In the closing paragraph of a letter for this activity, you should thank the reader for time spent reading the letter with an expression of desire to receive a favorable response. Add information of the enclosed Intent of Commitment form with due date to be mailed.

Leave a blank line after the salutation, between paragraphs, and before the complimentary close.

Table 2.1.6-2 Business Letter Format *(continued)*

Complimentary close
Respectfully yours,
Signature
Handwritten signature (for a mailed letter)
Typed name
Enc. (or Att.)

Table 2.1.6-3 Intent of Commitment Form

Name and title:	
Organization:	
Address:	
Telephone/Fax:	
Email address:	

Having been fully informed of the need for development of a health education program focusing on _____ (name of program or topic area) and targeted to _____ (identify intended audience), as a spokesperson for the listed organization, I am indicating the following areas where support and assistance can be offered to _____ (name of sponsoring agency/organization).

Check All That Apply	Types of Support
	Financial assistance
	Guest speakers
	Publicity

(continues)

Table 2.1.6-3 Intent of Commitment Form *(continued)*

	Other support not listed that can be offered (please explain in the space provided here)
Date:	**Signature:**

3. Checklist for contents in a letter to a potential stakeholder:
   a. Purpose or intent of letter
   b. Your name, title, and organization
   c. Target population for program planning
   d. Area of emphasis of program
   e. Justification of need for program
   f. Various types of support needed
   g. Solicitation of support from person to whom the letter is written
   h. Ways for the recipient to respond to seek additional information

COMPETENCY 2.2 DEVELOP GOALS AND OBJECTIVES

2.2.2 Identify Desired Outcomes Utilizing the Needs Assessment Results

Title Developing an Outcome Statement

Objective The student will be able to determine behavioral outcomes to be achieved prior to collecting data.

Directions

1. The Centers for Disease Control and Prevention (CDC) collects routine surveillance data on sexually transmitted diseases. Go to the CDC website (www.cdc.gov) to review data related to chlamydia. Find the latest data for Orlando, Florida. Note actual numbers, as well the rate of chlamydia, has risen during each of the surveillance years.

2. Read the following *scenario*.
   The Orlando Health Department has decided the increasing incidence of chlamydia is a priority health concern. However, before an effort is taken to undertake a needs assessment related to sexually transmitted infections, behavioral outcomes needed to affect a decrease in incidence should be developed.

3. Develop and record an outcome statement related to reducing behavioral risks related to chlamydia in **Table 2.2.2-1**.

4. Using **Table 2.2.2-1**, list four behaviors that increase the risk of infection and include needed changes in order to reduce the incidence of chlamydia in this community. Be sure they are directly related to the outcome statement.

Student Resources

1. The Centers for Disease Control and Prevention website provides information that can be used in this activity.
   http://www.cdc.gov

   a. Click on "C" in the A–Z index at the top of the page.

   b. Scroll down and click on "Chlamydia [*Chlamydia trachomatis* Disease]". Open the fact sheet to review the risks for chlamydia.

   c. Click on the "statistics" link in the green box to the left to review the statistics for chlamydia.

   d. Find data for Orlando, FL by typing "chlamydia data Orlando, FL" in the search box. Select the result for "Table 6."

   e. Use this information to write an outcome statement for **Step 3**.

2. The Community Health Status Indicators website can be used for finding information for Orlando, FL.
   http://communityhealth.hhs.gov
   In the drop lists on the left of the page, select "Current" for the year, "Florida" for the state, and "Orange" for the county (Orlando is located in Orange County, FL).

Table 2.2.2-1 Outcome Statement with Behavioral Changes to Reduce Incidence of Chlamydia

Outcome statement:	
Risk Behavior	**Behavior Change Goal with Justification**
1.	
2.	
3.	
4.	

2.2.6 Assess Resources Needed to Achieve Objectives

Title Resource Needs: Personnel and Tangible Items

Objective The student will be able to indicate resources needed to achieve program objectives.

Directions

1. Read the following *scenario*.
   The local Boys and Girls Club wants to improve intake of fruits and vegetables in its young people. Leaders of the club are collaborating with the local health department health educator, who will be providing educational materials and expertise for this project. The health educator has determined four classes are needed to teach the students about the importance of eating at least five servings of fruits and vegetables every day. Students will be given tools to track their progress for 1 month and will be rewarded for their efforts.
2. Develop and record in **Table 2.2.6-1** a list of personnel by job title or agency needed in the development of this program, taking into account such factors as skills in finance, budgeting, communication, administration, and publishing.
3. In **Table 2.2.6-1**, also create a list of the tangible resources needed for the development of this program, such as computer programs, classroom technology, paper, printing, and participant rewards.
4. Form a group and compare the lists. Can this program be developed and implemented adequately with these resources? Does someone or something need to be added to these lists?
5. Create a new list after discussion.

Student Resources

1. Information and resources are available for improving fruit and vegetable intake.
   http://www.fruitsandveggiesmatter.gov
2. The U.K. National Health Service has information on eating more fruits and vegetables.
   http://www.nhs.uk
   In the search box, type "fruits and vegetables."

Table 2.2.6-1 Resource Needs: Personnel and Tangible Resources

Personnel	Tangible Resources

COMPETENCY 2.3 SELECT OR DESIGN STRATEGIES AND INTERVENTIONS

2.3.2 Design Theory-Based Strategies and Interventions to Achieve Stated Objectives

Title Using a Theoretical Framework for Designing Strategies

Objective The student will be able to describe the role of theories in developing health promotion strategies.

Directions

1. Access *Theory at a Glance: A Guide for Health Promotion Practice* (2nd ed.) (U.S. DHHS, 2005) located at cancer.gov and review each of the following theories/models of behavior change: health belief model, theory of planned behavior, stages of change model, social cognitive theory, and diffusions of innovations theory.
2. Define the key concepts/constructs from each of the theories/models and apply these concepts to the development of strategies to increase physical activity of adults in the community by using **Table 2.3.2-1.**

Student Resource

Readings on each theory/model found in *Theory at a Glance: A Guide for Health Promotion Practice* (2nd ed.)
http://www.cancer.gov
To access the document, type "theory at a glance" in the search box.

Reference

United States Department of Health and Human Resources, National Institutes of Health, National Cancer Institute. (2005). *Theory at a glance: A guide for health promotion practice* (2nd ed.). Retrieved from http://www.cancer.gov/cancertopics/cancerlibrary/theory.pdf

Table 2.3.2-1 Application of Theory to Health Promotion Strategies

Key Concept	Definition	Suggested Strategy to Increase Physical Activity
Health belief model		
Theory of planned behavior		

(continues)

Table 2.3.2-1 Application of Theory to Health Promotion Strategies *(continued)*

Stages of change model		
Social cognitive theory		
Diffusion of innovations		

2.3.4 Comply with Legal and Ethical Principles in Designing Strategies and Interventions

Title Code of Ethics: Guidance for Higher Level Conduct for Health Educators

Objective The student will be able to describe ways to avoid legal and/or ethical violations concerning confidentiality, informed consent, and/or negligence.

Directions

1. Read the long version of the *Code of Ethics for the Health Education Profession* as published by the Coalition of National Health Education Organizations (1999) available at cnheo.org.
2. Read material about legal and ethical concerns, specifically confidentiality, informed consent, and negligence, provided by the course instructor.
3. Use **Table 2.3.4-1** to explain the guidance for higher level conduct given by the *Code of Ethics for the Health Education Profession* related to confidentiality, informed consent, and negligence. Cite one or more specific articles and sections and explain how upholding the specific standard could help a health educator avoid legal and/or ethical violations related to confidentiality, informed consent, and negligence.

Student Resource

Coalition of National Health Education Organizations. (1999). *Code of ethics for the health education profession*
http://www.cnheo.org

Reference

Coalition of National Health Education Organizations. (1999). *Code of ethics for the health education profession*. Retrieved from http://www.cnheo.org

Table 2.3.4-1 Code of Ethics Guidance on Confidentiality, Informed Consent, and Negligence

Legal/Ethical Concern	Article(s)	Section(s)	Explain Guidance Provided Related to the Ethical Concern
Confidentiality			
Informed consent			
Negligence			

2.3.5 Apply Principles of Cultural Competence in Selecting and Designing Strategies and Interventions

Title What's My Cultural Competence Quotient?

Objectives
1. The student will be able to identify cultural differences among groups.
2. The student will be able to apply appropriate interventions.

Directions
1. Select a cultural group from the following list:
   a. Sub-Saharan Africans
   b. African Americans
   c. Alaska Natives
   d. Arab Americans
   e. Asians
   f. Hispanics/Latinos
   g. Native Americans
   h. Pacific Islanders
   i. Eastern Europeans
2. Investigate the group selected in terms of health practices and beliefs, common health concerns, and cultural characteristics or barriers that might impact health prevention and treatment. Two excellent sources are listed in **Student Resources**.
3. Summarize some of the key findings in a bulleted list using the following *example* as a guide.

Example

Group: Muslims
Key findings:
- Family and religious community are very important
- Religious and social obligations are a priority over individualism
- Disease or ill health is an act of God
- Healing is an act of god
- Daily prayers and fasting are important traditions

Group:

Key findings:

4. Based upon the findings, outline appropriate strategies or interventions for a health promotion or disease prevention program for the group selected. It may be helpful to select a specific health issue as an example to formulate the response.

Use the following *example* as a guide.

Example

In a health promotion program for diabetic Muslims, the health educator needs to be aware of the dietary restrictions practiced by the Muslims. Fasting is an important part of Muslim religious practices, so balancing proper nutritional habits for a diabetic would need to fit into the practices. For example, some dietary guidelines to help control blood glucose levels during fasting can be recommended. Information about medications during fasting is needed. Same-gender instructors or health educators are encouraged.

Student Resources

1. Management Sciences for Health
   http://www.msh.org
   a. In the search box, type "Provider's Guide to Quality and Culture" and select the first result.
   b. Click on the "Go to Resource" link.
   c. The link to "Cultural Groups" is in the menu in the left column.
2. Centers for Disease Control and Prevention
   http://www.cdc.gov
   Type "Racial and Ethnic Minority Populations" in the search box.

2.3.6 Pilot Test Strategies and Interventions

Title Pretesting Health Education Strategies

Objective The student will be able to use formative evaluation techniques to pretest health education strategies.

Directions

1. Develop a one-page flyer promoting small steps to eating better and living a healthier life-style. The target population is employees at a manufacturing facility.
2. Test the readability of the flyer. Use the help function of word processing software to locate instructions for enabling readability statistics. A grade level of the written material will be provided. An eighth grade reading level is a general recommendation.
3. Revise the flyer, if needed, to achieve the desired readability of at least an eighth grade level.
4. Pretest the flyer by conducting a focus group to review the flyer and solicit comments. Gather four to six people who represent the target population. If this is not possible, conduct the focus group with classmates. Use the focus group guide located in **Table 2.3.6-1** to gather opinions about the flyer. Record focus group responses in the table.
5. If feedback from the pretest focus group indicates the need for improvement, revise the flyer to increase the likelihood of implementing a successful health promotion message.

Student Resource

University of Kansas Work Group for Community Health and Development. (2011). Conducting focus groups. Review Chapter 3, Section 6.
http://ctb.ku.edu

Reference

KU Work Group for Community Health and Development. (2011). Conducting focus groups. In: *The community tool box* (Chapter 3, Section 6). Lawrence: University of Kansas. Retrieved from http://ctb.ku.edu/en/tablecontents/section_1018.aspx

Table 2.3.6-1 Focus Group Guide for Pretest of Materials

Introduction: The purpose of this focus group is to get your opinions about a health promotion flyer.	
Questions	**Participant Responses**
Do you think the flyer is graphically appealing? If not, how could it be improved to make it more appealing?	
What is the main message of the flyer?	

Table 2.3.6-1 Focus Group Guide for Pretest of Materials *(continued)*

Do you think the message is clear and easy to understand? If not, how could it be improved to make it clearer?	
Do you think the message of the flyer will persuade an individual to take small steps toward eating better and living a healthier lifestyle? If not, how could the flyer be rewritten to be more persuasive?	
Do you think the flyer is appropriate to use with employees of a factory? Why or why not?	
Other question(s):	

COMPETENCY 2.4 DEVELOP A SCOPE AND SEQUENCE FOR THE DELIVERY OF HEALTH EDUCATION

2.4.1 Determine the Range of Health Education Needed to Achieve Goals and Objectives

Title HECAT to the Rescue: Designing Content for Workshop

Objective The student will be able to outline content needed to achieve listed objectives for a health education workshop.

Directions
1. Go to the CDC Healthy Youth! website listed in **Student Resources** and find the Health Education Curriculum Analysis Tool (HECAT). Review the site and become familiar with HECAT. Listed next are two objectives of HECAT and Standard One of the Alcohol and Other Drug Module for ninth through twelfth grade students.
   a. Differentiate between the proper use and abuse of over-the-counter medicines.
   b. Differentiate between the proper use and abuse of prescription medicines.
2. Work with a partner, and using the information in **Student Resources**, brainstorm the content that might be included in a 4-hour workshop or presentation to meet the two objectives.
   a. Create an outline of the content without a partner.
   b. Include time frames (how many minutes) for each section of the content.
   c. Use the *Sample* to get started.

Sample

Topic	Time Frame
I. Over-the-counter medicines	2 hours total
A. Types of OTC drugs	30 minutes
1.	
2.	
B. Proper use of OTC drugs	
C. Misuse of OTC drugs	
1.	
II. Prescription medicines	
A.	
B.	

Student Resources
1. National Association of School Nurses. *Drugs of abuse.* Several educational programs dealing with prescription drug abuse are available.
   www.nasn.org
   Look for "Smart Move: Smart Choices."
2. U.S. Food and Drug Administration. *Drugs. Resources for You. Information for Consumers*
   http://www.fda.gov
   "Medicines in My Home" is an example of a curriculum about OTC medicines.
3. Centers for Disease Control and Prevention
   www.cdc.gov
   Type "HECAT" or "Health education curriculum analysis tool" in the search box and click on the Search button. Look for the content called, "Modules."

2.4.2 Select Resources Required to Implement Health Education

Title Are These Materials Right for This Cultural Group?

Objective The student will be able to select resources and materials appropriate for diverse cultures.

Directions

1. Select a specific cultural group from the list that follows. The group can be the same one used in **Activity 2.3.5**.
   a. Sub-Saharan Africans
   b. African Americans
   c. Alaska Natives
   d. Arab Americans
   e. Asians
   f. Hispanics/Latinos
   g. Native Americans
   h. Pacific Islanders
   i. Eastern Europeans
2. Search the Internet to locate health education, health promotion, or disease prevention materials that are culturally appropriate for the group selected. Many volunteer health agencies provide culturally appropriate health education material. Find at least three sources for the selected group.
3. Record in **Table 2.4.2-1** information describing sources with appropriate materials for the selected cultural group.

Student Resources

1. Management Sciences for Health
   http://www.msh.org
   a. In the search box, type "Provider's Guide to Quality and Culture" and select the first result.
   b. Click on the "Go to Resource" link.
   c. Look for the link to "Cultural Groups" in the menu in the left column.
2. Centers for Disease Control and Prevention, Office of Minority Health and Health Disparities
   http://www.cdc.gov
   In search box, type "minority health resources."
3. National Prevention Information Network (NPIN)
   http://www.cdcnpin.org
   Look for the link to "Communities at Risk" in the left column menu.

Table 2.4.2-1 Sources with Relevant Resources for Selected Cultural Group

Cultural Group	Instructor Resources (Cost and Type)	Participant Resources (Cost, Type, Readability Level, Language, and Target Audience)
Source		
Source		
Source		

2.4.3 Use Logic Models to Guide the Planning Process

Title Translating Objectives into a Logic Model

Objective The student will be able to develop a logic model based upon process and outcome objectives of a health promotion program.

Directions
1. Read suggested material on logic models in **Student Resources**.
2. Complete **Table 2.4.3-1** by defining each of the following components of a logic model: inputs, activities, outputs, short-term outcomes, intermediate outcomes, and long-term outcomes.
3. Translate the given process and outcome objectives into logic model components using **Table 2.4.3-2**.

Student Resources
1. Centers for Disease Control and Prevention. (2008, December). *Logic model basics, ETA evaluation briefs, No. 2.* Available from http://www.cdc.gov
   This can be located by searching for "logic model basics."
2. University of Kansas, Work Group for Community Health and Development. (2011). Developing a logic model or theory of change. In: *The community tool box* (Chapter 2, Section 1). Available from http://ctb.ku.edu/en/tablecontents/section_1877.aspx

Table 2.4.3-1 Definition of Logic Model Components

Logic Model Component	Definition
Inputs	
Activities	
Outputs	
Short-term outcomes	
Intermediate outcomes	
Long-term outcomes	

Table 2.4.3-2 Translation of Program Objectives into a Logic Model

Goal: To reduce the incidence of oral disease in County Z
Long-term outcome objective: Within 5 years, reduce the percentage of children ages 4–12 in County Z who suffer from untreated dental decay from X% (baseline) to Y%.
Long-term outcome:
Intermediate outcome objective: By (month/year), increase to Y% the percentage of children ages 4–12 in County Z who received a professional dental screening in the past year.

Table 2.4.3-2 Translation of Program Objectives into a Logic Model *(continued)*

Intermediate outcome:
Intermediate outcome objective: By (month/year), increase to Y% the percentage of children ages 4–12 in County Z who had dental sealants applied to their molar teeth.
Intermediate outcome:
Short-term outcome objective: By (month/year), X% of primary care clinicians in pediatric and/or family practices will report referring to a dentist those children ages 4–12 in County Z who had signs of early decay or high risk for future oral disease.
Short-term outcome:
Short-term outcome objective: By (month/year), X% of primary care clinicians in pediatric and/or family practices will report providing brief education about the importance of routine dental screening to parents of children ages 4–12 in County Z.
Short-term outcome:
Process objective: By (month/year), program staff will provide X number of medical education forums designed to increase primary care clinicians' perceived importance of oral disease and intention to refer children for routine dental screening.
Inputs: Activities: Outputs:

2.4.6 Analyze the Opportunity for Integrating Health Education into Other Programs

Title Policy and Environmental Analysis of Health Education Activities in School Environments

Objective The student will be able to use tools to assess health education activities in specific settings.

Directions

1. The following topics are addressed in the CDC's Community Health Assessment aNd Group Evaluation (CHANGE) tool in **Student Resource**.
2. Access the Centers for Disease Control and Prevention. Use the CDC search box to find the Healthy Communities Program (the steps are also described in **Student Resource**). Open the Healthy Communities Program page and look for the Tools and Resources section. Select "CHANGE Tool and Action Guide." In the left column menu, click on "CHANGE Downloads" to retrieve the School Sector files needed for this activity. Scroll down to Action Step 3 and select the School Sector. This will open an Excel file.
3. Click on any of the tabs to select one of the following topics for this activity: nutrition, physical activity, chronic disease management, after school, or district.
4. Review the Policy and Environment table for the topic selected. Close this file.
5. Go back to Action Step 3 and open the School Sector under "Examples for questions for each sector." This is PDF. Scroll down to find the topic selected in **Step 3**.
6. Review the questions listed for the topic selected.
7. With the help of the instructor, select any secondary school, middle school, or elementary school (public or private). Try to select one with a quality website.
8. Gather the information for the questions from **Step 5** ("Examples for questions for each sector") for the school selected. Most of the information should be available at the school's website. Try to find the answers to as many questions as possible. Don't worry if all of the needed information is not on the school website. (Contact the school through email or phone to obtain the information needed if you are comfortable doing so.)
9. Create a chart or table to record findings. Include the school name, the topic, the questions asked, and the Policy and Environment response number for each question as shown in the following *sample*.

Sample
School: Lilly Washington High School

Questions and Scores
Implement a referral system to help students access tobacco cessation resources or services?

Score: Policy = 2 Problem identification/gaining agenda status; Environment = 1 Elements not in place

10. In a short paragraph, summarize the strengths and weaknesses of the school in addressing the topic selected. Also provide an evaluation of the CHANGE Tool's value in analyzing policies and the environment for a school or other sectors.

Student Resource
Centers for Disease Control and Prevention
http://www.cdc.gov
   a. In the search box, type "Healthy Communities Program." Select the first result.
   b. Under Tools and Resources, click on "CHANGE Tool and Action Guide" to go to the Community Health Assessment aNd Group Evaluation (CHANGE) page.
   c. In the far left column, click on "CHANGE downloads" to access both the Excel and PDF Questions file needed for this activity.

2.4.7 Develop a Process for Integrating Health Education into Other Programs

Title Integrating Health Education into Existing Programs

Objective The student will be able to outline procedures for integrating health education into specific settings.

Directions
1. **Activity 2.4.6** must be completed before attempting this activity.
2. Refer to the results of **Activity 2.4.6**. Review weaknesses found from the policy and environment analysis of the school for the selected topic.
3. Use **Student Resources** or Internet resources found to determine ways school personnel could improve the situation by integrating the selected topic into existing programs or components of the school day.
4. Review the following *Sample*.
   In **Activity 2.4.6**, Lilly Washington High School had low scores in both policy and environment concerning resources or services in place for tobacco cessation. To improve the situation, school personnel could contact the American Lung Association to offer the Not On Tobacco (N-O-T) program (American Lung Association, 2008). This is a 10-week voluntary smoking cessation program for high school students. The program could be offered as part of an after-school activity.
5. Add slides to the slide show developed in **Activity 2.4.6** with recommendations for school personnel to improve the selected topic weakness in policy and environment.

Student Resources
1. Alliance for a Healthier Generation
   http://www.healthiergeneration.org/default.aspx
2. Model School Wellness Policies
   http://www.schoolwellnesspolicies.org
3. Healthy Kids, Healthy Schools
   http://www.healthykidshealthyschools.org

Reference
American Lung Association. (2008). *Not on tobacco (N-O-T)*. Retrieved from
   http://www.notontobacco.com

COMPETENCY 2.5 ADDRESS FACTORS THAT AFFECT IMPLEMENTATION

2.5.1 Identify Factors that Foster or Hinder Implementation

Title Factors of Successful Program Implementation

Objective The student will be able to list steps of successful program implementation.

Directions

1. Review the partial list of factors that have been identified as influencing the success of health education program implementation.
   a. Adoption
   b. Stakeholders
   c. Resources
   d. Training
   e. Support of administration or management
2. Search ERIC or the Internet for articles or websites that describe the role of one or more of the aforementioned factors listed in successful health education programs. Use phrases such as *role of resources in successful health promotion programs* or *role of stakeholders in successful health promotion programs* in the search.
3. Describe the program reviewed in a paragraph. Include the reference for the information retrieved, and explain the role of the factor(s) selected in the overall success of the program reviewed.

Student Resources

1. National Prevention Information Network
   http://www.cdcnpin.org
   Once at the main page look for the link to HIV/AIDS and then the link to Elements of Successful Programs.
2. National Registry of Evidence-based Programs and Practices
   http://www.nrepp.samhsa.gov
   Use the link for View All Interventions or type in the name of a health issue in the search box.

2.5.2 Analyze Factors that Foster or Hinder Implementation

Title Analyzing the Implementation of a Work Site Smoke-Free Policy

Objective The student will be able to analyze obstacles or barriers that impact program implementation.

Directions

1. Read the following *scenario.*

   In September, the owner of a large company decided that the work site would become a smoke-free environment at the beginning of the new year. His decision was based on the fact that he had just lost an uncle to lung cancer as a result of smoking. To implement the new policy, the owner sent a memo to department managers informing them of the decision, instructed them to post information to alert employees of the change along with penalties for violating the policy, begin removing all ashtrays from the break rooms, and display no-smoking signs throughout the work site.

2. Assume the role of a health educator employed by the company. Prepare a memo to the owner outlining concerns for the method of implementation for the new policy and provide reasons why it may fail.

3. Use materials found in **Student Resources** to offer suggestions for a more successful implementation process in the same memo.

Student Resources

1. Centers for Disease Control and Prevention
   http://www.cdc.gov
   Type "tobacco-free campus toolkit" in the search box.
2. National Business Group on Health
   http://www.businessgrouphealth.org
   Click on the Tobacco Cessation link and then on the Worksite Programs and Policies link.

2.5.3 Use Findings of Pilot to Refine Implementation Plans as Needed

Title A Pilot Test of a Podcast

Objective The student will be able to refine implementation plans based upon a pilot test of a health education strategy.

Directions
1. Develop a 4–6-minute script for a podcast for one of the following topics targeting college students:
   a. How to correctly use a condom
   b. How to eat healthy with little money
   c. How to effectively manage time
   d. How to have a healthy relationship
2. Audio record the podcast using instructions provided by the course instructor.
3. Pilot test the podcast with 3–5 people from the target audience and record comments about the podcast in **Table 2.5.3-1**.
4. Modify the content of the podcast based upon feedback from the pilot. Then create a revised podcast.

Student Resources
1. Computer software to create and publish a podcast
2. Instructions from the course instructor about how to create a podcast

Table 2.5.3-1 Target Audience Feedback from Pilot Test

Feedback Question	Response
Was the length of the podcast appropriate?	
What were the main points of the podcast?	
Were the main points of the podcast understandable? If not, how could the message be improved?	
Was the sound quality of the podcast appropriate? If not, how could the sound be improved?	
Is a podcast an appropriate method for disseminating the message for the target population? Why or why not?	

2.5.4 Develop a Conducive Learning Environment

Title Psychological and Physical Characteristics Conducive to Learning

Objective The student will be able to identify steps for developing a psychological and physical environment that is conducive to learning.

Directions
1. Read material about characteristics of learning environments provided by the course instructor.
2. Identify psychological and physical characteristics that must be considered in efforts to develop an environment conducive to learning. Record responses in **Table 2.5.4-1**.
3. Distinguish among characteristics listed in **Table 2.5.4-1** that are appropriate to tasks a health educator should take before, during, and after an intervention to ensure an environment that is conducive to learning. Create the checklist by completing **Table 2.5.4-2**.

Student Resource
Reading material regarding general principles of learning to be provided by the instructor.

Table 2.5.4-1 Psychological and Physical Characteristics of Environments Conducive to Learning

Psychological Characteristics	Physical Characteristics

Table 2.5.4-2 Tasks to Create an Environment Conducive to Learning Before, During, and After Intervention

Tasks before intervention	1.
	2.
	3.
	4.

(continues)

Table 2.5.4-2 Tasks to Create an Environment Conducive to Learning Before, During, and After Intervention *(continued)*

Tasks during intervention	1.
	2.
	3.
	4.
Tasks after intervention	1.
	2.
	3.
	4.

Implement Health Education

INTRODUCTION

Once the planning process is complete, the implementing phase begins. This chapter has 15 entry-level sub-competencies with one activity per sub-competency in Area of Responsibility III.

Students will be asked to practice specific skills through a variety of tasks. One task requires students to create interview questions to use in an actual interview with a practicing professional. The interview focus is to assess skills needed to work collaboratively with other professionals and organizations in implementing new programs. The professional will be asked to identify characteristics to consider when providing training services.

Scenarios are provided to help students through the process of determining the capacity to implement a program by pairing program goals and objectives with appropriate organizations and individuals in a specific community. Also, students will examine baseline data relevant to program implementation. Students will practice the process of revising objectives during program implementation and how to write a midyear budget report for a grant to demonstrate the appropriate use of resources.

Topics such as physical activity among adults, adolescent obesity, conflict resolution, and inhalant abuse are used to explore evidence-based interventions for delivering health promotion programs to specific cultural groups. Students will practice creating tailored messages using technology such as podcasts, blogs, and social networking. As a result of an activity in this chapter, students will document the completion of training in human subjects in research that can be used in their portfolios or resumes.

For this text, please go to the student companion website at **go.jblearning.com/PracticalApp** to complete activities using e-templates, and then pass your completed activities to your instructor for review or grading.

COMPETENCY 3.1 IMPLEMENT A PLAN OF ACTION

3.1.1 Assess Readiness for Implementation

Title Determining Capacity to Implement a Program

Objective The student will be able to pair program goals and objectives with appropriate organizations and individuals, facilitating capacity building when necessary.

Directions

1. Review the information on capacity building in **Student Resources**.
2. Read the following *scenario*.

   A needs assessment of an urban community with a large Hispanic population reveals a high rate of overweight and obesity in young people aged 10–14. The health educator at the local health department is promoting a goal to reduce the rates of overweight and obesity in this city. A program has been developed that includes health and physical education in the schools, identifying students who meet the Centers for Disease Control and Prevention (CDC) criteria for overweight and obesity, and an after school program on nutrition and fitness. This program will be pilot tested in one city middle school. This particular school gathers data every school year on weight, height, and BMI of each student. Objectives include but are not limited to the following list.

   The students at the middle school will be able to:
   a. Compare calorie contents of various foods
   b. Explain adequate calorie intake for ideal body weight
   c. Justify importance of eating five servings of fruits and vegetables each day
   d. Record caloric intake, fruit and vegetable intake, and exercise daily for 1 week
   e. Participate in a group fitness class after school 5 days a week for 30 minutes
3. The local health department's health educator understands that other people, organizations and institutions will need to be involved in the successful implementation of this program. In **Table 3.1.1-1**, first identify key personnel in the school system, health department, family resource/youth service centers, and community who can be involved in implementation of this program. Second, identify assets key personnel can offer with areas of expertise, time, equipment, space, financial support, supplies, as well as other forms of support. Third, match key personnel with potential contributions listed in **Step 2** that will meet one or more objectives necessary for successful program implementation.

Student Resources

1. Southern Rural Development Center houses Lionel Beaulieu's *Mapping the assets of your community: A key component for building local capacity*. Publication No. 227. http://srdc.msstate.edu
2. The Academy of Nutrition and Dietetics (AND) has nutrition information. www.eatright.org

Table 3.1.1-1 Capacity Building for Weight Reduction in Teens

List Key Personnel for Each Category	What Assets Can Key Personnel Bring or Contribute to the Implementation of This Program?	Which Objectives Fit Best with Contributions Available from Potential Key Personnel?
School		
Health department		

Table 3.1.1-1 Capacity Building for Weight Reduction in Teens *(continued)*

Parents		
Family resource/youth service center		
Parks and recreation department		
After school programs		
YMCA		
Other (identify)		

3.1.2 Collect Baseline Data

Title Determining What Information Is Needed to Implement a Program

Objective The student will be able examine baseline data relevant to the program being implemented.

Directions

1. Read **Activity 3.1.1** to be familiar with the program goal of reducing overweight and obesity in 10- to 14-year-old students in an urban middle school. Also, carefully review the objectives for the program.
2. Review data sources that include information on overweight and obesity that can be found in **Student Resources**.
3. Answer the questions in **Table 3.1.2-1** using data available from the Centers for Disease Control and Prevention (CDC) website.
4. Develop an informational letter to parents using items from the following list. It should not be so lengthy that the reader may dispose of it without reading the entire letter.
   a. Describe the type, length of time, and location of the program.
   b. Ask for parental/guardian consent for their child to participate in the program.
   c. Identify the program goal and objectives.
   d. Explain the purpose for the letter.
   e. Provide a brief description of both short- and long-term obesity and overweight risks.

Table 3.1.2-1 CDC Data on Overweight and Obesity in Persons Ages 10–14 Years

Questions related to overweight and obesity in persons ages 10–14 years
For each answer provided, identify the year the data was gathered by CDC.
1. What is the rate of overweight and obesity in 10–14-year-olds in the United States?
2. What minority group has the highest rate of overweight and obesity? What is the rate?
3. What state has the highest rate of overweight and obesity in 10–14-year-olds? What is the rate?
4. What state has the lowest rate of overweight and obesity in 10–14-year-olds? What is the rate?

Table 3.1.2-2 Program Data to Document Weight Reduction in Age Group 10–14 Years

Data Type	Baseline Data and Date	During Program Data and Date
Weight in pounds		
Height in inches		
BMI		
Other:		
Other:		
Other:		

    f. Ask parents/guardians for consent for obtaining the child's height, weight, and BMI information.

    g. Explain who is sponsoring the program and the cost of it.

    h. Provide a means of contact for further information needed by the parents/guardians.

5. Use **Table 3.1.2-2** to identify additional data to be collected at the beginning and during program implementation that will identify changes in overweight and obesity.

Student Resources

1. The Academy of Nutrition and Dietetics (AND) has nutrition information.
www.eatright.org

2. The CDC has data related to rates of overweight and obesity.
www.cdc.gov
Type "overweight and obesity" in the search box.

3. Data on attitudes and behaviors in youth related to obesity and diabetes can be found at the Youth Risk Behavior Surveillance System (YRBSS) website.
http://www.cdc.gov
Use the A–Z Index to locate the relevant information.

4. Information on overweight and obesity (BMI) prevalence and trends data can be found at the Behavioral Risk Factor Surveillance System (BRFSS) home page. Use the A–Z Index to locate.
http://www.cdc.gov

3.1.3 Use Strategies to Ensure Cultural Competence in Implementing Health Education Plans

Title Plain and Simple: Improve Health Literacy

Objectives
1. The student will be able to identify practical strategies to improve health literacy.
2. The student will be able to explain practical strategies to improve health literacy.

Directions
1. Access the National Institutes of Health (NIH) (U.S. DHHS, 2010a) website (nih.gov), enter the text, "health literacy" in the search box, and click on the Search button. Locate the link titled "Clear Communication: An NIH Health Literacy Initiative" and click on it.
2. Define health literacy and list the range of abilities needed for health literacy using **Table 3.1.3-1**.
3. Access the web document *Health Literacy Online: A Guide to Designing and Writing Easy-to-Use Health Web Sites* (U.S. DHHS, 2010b) at health.gov by typing the document title into the search box. Read the section titled, "Write Actionable Content."
4. Write a one-sentence explanation and give at least one example for each of the strategies listed in **Table 3.1.3-2**. These strategies are designed to make health education content actionable. Record the responses in **Table 3.1.3-2**.
5. Select health education content from two of the following small media formats:
   a. Blog
   b. Brochure/pamphlet
   c. Podcast
   d. Video sharing (e.g., YouTube)
   e. Website
6. Review the health education content of the chosen media and using the strategies presented in **Table 3.1.3-2**. Rate the extent to which each strategy for making the content actionable is achieved based on a scale from 1 to 3 (1 = not achieved, needs major improvement; 2 = partially achieved, but needs improvement; and 3 = achieved very well, no improvement needed).
7. Record ratings of the two chosen media in **Table 3.1.3-3**, and for each rating in which improvement is needed, provide practical suggestions for making the content more actionable and thus improving health literacy.

Table 3.1.3-1 Health Literacy: A Definition and List of Individual Abilities Needed

Definition with Citation of Source	Individual Abilities Needed
	1.
	2.
	3.

Table 3.1.3-2 Strategies for Developing Actionable Health Education Content

Strategy for Making Content Actionable	One-Sentence Explanation with Example(s)
Put the most important information first.	
Describe the health behavior—just the basics.	
Include benefits of taking action.	
Provide specific action steps.	
Write in plain language.	
Check content for accuracy.	

Table 3.1.3-3 Assessment of Written Health Education Content: Is It Actionable?

Strategy for Making Content Actionable	Extent to Which the Strategy Is Achieved (1 = not achieved, major improvement needed; 2 = partially achieved, but needs improvement; and 3 = achieved very well, no improvement needed)	Suggestions for Making Content More Actionable (If Applicable)
Chosen media No. 1		
Put the most important information first.		
Describe the health behavior—just the basics.		
Stay positive and realistic. Include benefits of taking action.		

Table 3.1.3-3 Assessment of Written Health Education Content: Is It Actionable? *(continued)*

Provide specific action steps.		
Write in plain language.		
Check content for accuracy.		
Chosen media No. 2		
Put the most important information first.		
Describe the health behavior—just the basics.		
Stay positive and realistic. Include benefits of taking action.		
Provide specific action steps.		
Write in plain language.		
Check content for accuracy.		

Student Resources

1. United States Department of Health and Human Resources, National Institutes of Health. (2010). *Clear communication: An NIH health literacy initiative.*
   Available at www.nih.gov
   In the search box, type the title of the document.
2. United States Department of Health and Human Resources, Office of Disease Prevention and Health Promotion. (2010). *Health literacy online: A guide to writing and designing easy-to-use health web sites.*
   www.health.gov
   a. Go to the health.gov website; under "HHS initiatives," select "Health Communications, Health Literacy & e-Health."
   b. Click on "Health Literacy" in the left column menu.
   c. Scroll down to find the link in the middle of the page.

References

United States Department of Health and Human Resources, National Institutes of Health. (2010a). *Clear communication: An NIH health literacy initiative.* Retrieved from http://www.nih.gov/clearcommunication/healthliteracy.htm

United States Department of Health and Human Resources, Office of Disease Prevention and Health Promotion. (2010b). *Health literacy online: A guide to writing and designing easy-to-use health web sites.* Washington, DC: Author. Retrieved from www.health.gov/healthliteracyonline

3.1.4 Use a Variety of Strategies to Deliver a Plan of Action

Title Multiple Strategies and Technology in Delivering Health Promotion Interventions

Objectives
1. The student will be able to identify a variety of evidence-based interventions for health promotion.
2. The student will be able to identify potential uses of technology in the delivery of health promotion interventions.

Directions
1. Select a topic from the following list:
   a. Cancer
   b. Diabetes
   c. Family planning
   d. Maternal, infant, and child health
   e. Physical activity
2. Access the Healthy People 2020 website (healthypeople.gov). Select the tab titled "2020 Topics & Objectives," locate and select the link for the chosen topic, and then select the tab titled, "Interventions & Resources."
3. The task is to use a mix of strategies targeting multiple impacts on health behavior including the individual, interpersonal relationships, organizations, community, and environmental and/or policy change. Review the evidenced-based community interventions for the chosen topic. Select at least four interventions and identify the level of focus (e.g., individual, interpersonal, organizational, community, environmental/policy change) and provide a brief description of each intervention. Record responses in **Table 3.1.4-1**.
4. Review material about uses of Web 2.0 tools (e.g., blogs, podcasts, feeds, social networking sites, video sharing, and wikis) and other technology (e.g., short, enhanced, or multimedia message service) for delivering health education interventions. Some sources are listed in **Student Resources**.
5. Select one of the interventions listed in **Table 3.1.4-1**. Identify potential uses of Web 2.0 technology and/or other technologies in the delivery of the selected intervention. Give specific examples of ways in which the technology could be used in delivering the intervention. Record responses in **Table 3.1.4-2** using the example provided in the table.

Table 3.1.4-1 Multilevel Evidence-Based Interventions

Evidence-Based Community Intervention	Level of Focus (Individual, Interpersonal, Organizational, Community, Environmental/Policy Change)	Brief Description of Intervention

(continues)

Table 3.1.4-1 Multilevel Evidence-Based Interventions *(continued)*

Table 3.1.4-2 Use of Technology in Delivering Health Promotion Interventions

Selected Intervention	Specific Examples of Use of Technology in the Intervention
Example: Person-to-person interventions to improve caregivers' parenting skills	Example: To enhance caregivers' skills, set up a blog in which the health educator posts information about specific topics, such as teen sexual behavior. The blog can be used to provide guidance on how to approach talking to teens about the topic. Caregivers can respond to blog posts with questions and/or ideas. The health educator and caregivers can have an ongoing dialogue.

Student Resources

1. Healthy People 2020.
   www.healthypeople.gov
2. Burke, S., & Snyder, S. (2008). YouTube: An innovative learning resource for college health education courses. *International Electronic Journal of Health Education, 11*, 39–46.
3. Hanson, C., Thackeray, R., Barnes, M., Neiger, B., & McIntyre, E. (2008). Integrating Web 2.0 in health education preparation and practice. *American Journal of Health Education, 39* (3), 157–166.
4. Oomen-Early, J., & Burke, S. (2007). Entering the blogosphere: Blogs as teaching and learning tools in health education. *International Electronic Journal of Health Education, 10*, 186–196.

3.1.5 Promote Plan of Action

Title Promote Programs Using Tailored Messages

Objective The student will be able to outline a plan for promoting a program using personalization tactics for tailoring messages.

Directions
1. Before beginning this activity, complete the activity for **Sub-competency 2.3.5**, "Apply principles of cultural competence in selecting and designing strategies and interventions."
2. Read the article listed in **Student Resources** to gain understanding of using tailored messages in communicating about health.
3. Describe and provide an example of the three tactics for using the personalization strategy of tailoring in **Table 3.1.5-1**.
4. Outline a plan using the personalization tactics for a tailored promotion of the strategy or intervention developed for a specific cultural group from the activity for **Sub-competency 2.3.5**. Record the responses in **Table 3.1.5-2**. Use this *example* as a guide.

Example
1. *Target population:* Diabetic Muslims
2. *Strategy for target population*: Providing recommended dietary guidelines to help control blood glucose levels during fasting
3. *Media used for promotion:* Email and/or text message
4. *Personalization*: Identify in the email or text message the person's name
5. *Raising expectations*: State in the email or text message, "This program was developed for you with your needs in mind."
6. *Contextualization*: State in the email or text message, "This session will provide an opportunity for you to meet with a female health educator to learn ways to control blood glucose levels during fasting."

Student Resources
1. Completed activities for **Sub-competency 2.3.5**.
2. Hawkins, R. P., Kreuter, M., Resnicow, K., Fishbein, M., & Dijkstra, A. (2008). Understanding tailoring in communicating about health. *Health Education Research, 23* (3), 454–466.

Table 3.1.5-1 Tailored Strategy of Personalization: Three Tactics

Tactics of Personalization	Description and Examples of the Tactic
Identification	
Raising expectations	
Contextualization	

Table 3.1.5-2 Plan for Promotion Using Personalization Tactics to Tailor Messages

1. Target population	
2. Strategy for target population	
3. Media used for promotion	
4. Personalization	
5. Raising expectations	
6. Contextualization	

3.1.6 Apply Theories and Models of Implementation

Title Select Best Matching Theories

Objectives

1. The student will be able to select a theory to apply to a situation and determine if the chosen theory is appropriate for the given situation.
2. The student will be able to determine if the chosen theory is appropriate for the given situation.

Directions

1. Conduct a literature search to identify possible contributors to or reasons for low levels of physical activity among adults in the community.
2. Use **Table 3.1.6-1** to record the possible reasons for lack of physical activity. Then identify the level of interaction of these reasons (intrapersonal, interpersonal, community, or all three).
3. Complete the activities for **Sub-competency 2.3.2**, "Design theory-based strategies and interventions to achieve stated objectives."
4. Select two theories that are the best matches to serve as a guide for implementation of interventions to change the level of physical activity among adults. Justify the selected theories by answering the questions outlined in **Table 3.1.6-2**.

Student Resource

United States Department of Health and Human Resources, National Institutes of Health, National Cancer Institute. (2005). *Theory at a glance: A guide for health promotion practice.* http://www.cancer.gov
Type the document name in the search box.

Table 3.1.6-1 Reasons for Low Levels of Physical Activity Among Adults in the Community

Reasons	Level of Interaction (Intrapersonal, Interpersonal, Community, or All Three)

Table 3.1.6-2 Explanation for Best Matching Theories

Theory selection No. 1	
Is it appropriate for the level of interaction of the reasons in this situation? Explain.	
Is it logical given the reasons being addressed? Explain.	
Can all of the key concepts of the theory be used as a guide for program implementation in this situation? Explain.	
Theory selection No. 2	
Is it appropriate for the level of interaction of the reasons in this situation? Explain.	
Is it logical given the reasons being addressed? Explain.	
Can all of the key concepts of the theory be used as a guide for program implementation in this situation? Explain.	

3.1.7 Launch Plan of Action

Title Working with Others to Implement Programs

Objectives

1. The student will be able to identify the skills needed to work with others to implement a plan of action.
2. The student will be able to assess the skills needed to implement a plan of action.

Directions

1. Review material provided by the instructor about skills needed to work with others to implement a program, for example, communication skills, coalition building, community organizing, group dynamics, group facilitation, meeting planning, leadership, and conflict management.
2. Develop a list of at least 10 questions to be asked of either a leader of a community coalition focused on a health issue or a health educator who works collaboratively with others to implement programs. The questions should be written to improve your understanding of the specific skills needed to work with others to implement a program.
   Examples: What do you think are the keys to building a successful coalition? What steps do you take to assure that meetings run efficiently?
3. Obtain instructor approval of the questions.
4. Make arrangements to interview (via telephone or person to person) either a leader of a community coalition or a health educator who works collaboratively with others to implement programs. When requesting an interview, explain the purpose of the interview. See the course instructor for a list of local contacts for this activity.
5. Send the interviewee a copy of the interview guide a few days before the interview.
6. Conduct the interview.
7. Within 3 days after the interview, send a thank-you note to the interviewee.
8. Obtain from the instructor a list of local or regional community coalitions addressing a health issue. Attend one local community coalition meeting to observe characteristics outlined in the list of questions developed in **Step 2** and approved by the instructor. The purpose of attending a coalition meeting is to observe the group dynamics, stakeholder roles, meeting facilitation, conflict management, leadership, and other characteristics of the group process.
9. Use findings from the interview and the observations of a local community coalition to write a one-page summary of findings. The summary should include answers to the interview questions, specific examples of the skills or processes that were observed in the coalition meeting, and a description of the major strengths and challenges of working together to implement a program.

Student Resources

1. Reading material provided by the instructor
2. List of local community coalition leaders and/or health educators who work collaboratively with others to implement programs

COMPETENCY 3.2 MONITOR IMPLEMENTATION OF HEALTH EDUCATION

3.2.1 Monitor Progress in Accordance with Timeline

Title Creating a Program Implementation Plan Timeline

Objective The student will be able to arrange program tasks on a timeline.

Directions

1. Review the following list of randomly arranged tasks required to plan and implement a health promotion program.
   a. Write a rationale to justify the program.
   b. Conduct a community analysis.
   c. Hire/train staff for the program.
   d. Design an evaluation plan.
   e. Develop interventions and materials.
   f. Implement the program.
   g. Write an evaluation report.
   h. Identify funding source and obtain a proposal application.
   i. Collect baseline data for program evaluation.
   j. Prepare and distribute informed consent forms.
   k. Register participants.
   l. Create a marketing plan.
   m. Collect postprogram data to evaluate the program.
   n. Acquire equipment needed for the program.
   o. Assess target group needs.
   p. Write goals/objectives.
   q. Design marketing materials.
   r. Review literature about the topic.
   s. Establish dates for the program.
   t. Market the program.
   u. Establish a site for the program; reserve needed space.
   v. Analyze evaluation data.
2. Consider grouping tasks. For example, the marketing tasks (create a marketing plan, design marketing materials, market the program) could be considered a logical group.
3. Arrange and record the list in order of tasks that need to be completed first, second, and so on to successfully implement the program by completing **Table 3.2.1-1**.
4. Create a chart or table that would help in monitoring the progress toward completing the tasks listed. For convenience, use a 12-month, January-to-December hypothetical planning time frame. The chart or table should include recommended time frames for completion of each task and space to record when the tasks are started and completed. See **Table 3.2.1-2**.

Table 3.2.1-1 Logical Order of Tasks for Program Planning and Implementation

Logical Order of Tasks	Description of Task from Provided List
1.	
2.	
3.	
4.	
5.	

Table 3.2.1-1 Logical Order of Tasks for Program Planning and Implementation *(continued)*

6.	
7.	
8.	
9.	
10.	
11.	
12.	
13.	
14.	
15.	
16.	
17.	
18.	
19.	
20.	
21.	
22.	

Table 3.2.1-2 Sample of Partial Table

Task	Recommended Time Frame Dates	Date Started	Date Completed
Community analysis	January 1–February 1		
Market the program	July 15–August 1		
Write evaluation report	December 15–December 25		

Student Resources

1. Centers for Disease Control and Prevention
   http://www.cdc.gov
   Type the word "Timelines" in the search box. Scroll to find the link for "Social Networks Demonstration Project." A sample of a timeline is in this guide.
2. Most health education professional preparation books will have sections that explain timelines. Some specific terms associated with timelines include simple timelines, Gantt charts, program evaluation and review charts, and critical path analysis.

3.2.2 Assess Progress in Achieving Objectives

Title Exit Interview

Objective The student will be able to create an exit interview to assess process objectives.

Directions
1. Read the following *scenario*.

   The student wellness committee of the parent–teacher association (PTA) for a local middle school is implementing a workshop specifically designed for teacher aides and bus drivers. The four-session workshop focus is on ways to respond to bullying issues that have recently become an increasing problem. Based on past experiences with this target group, the committee is aware of the challenges with attendance and participation. Therefore, the committee created specific process objectives to help monitor and support attendance and participation. The process objectives are listed next.

   a. At the end of the first session, at least 75% of the participants interviewed will be satisfied with the workshop format (beginning and ending time frame, hourly schedule, breaks, food).

   b. At the end of the second session, all participants interviewed will feel comfortable in participating in workshop role-playing activities.

   c. At the end of the third session at least 85% of the participants interviewed will agree that they will return to the last session.

2. The committee agreed to use an exit interview as each session ends to assess the process objectives. Program facilitators will ask the participants to respond to several questions. The purpose of the exit interview is to assess whether the objectives are being met and to provide feedback to make changes for the following day's session.

3. Write at least three questions that could be used in the exit interview for each of the three sessions. Be sure to review the aforementioned objectives as a guide.

Student Resources
1. RHRC Consortium Monitoring and Evaluation Tool Kit. (2004). *Client exit protocol.*
   http://www.rhrc.org
   Type "exit interview" into the search box.
2. Centre for Health Service Development. (2011). *Care planning sub-program: Exit interview report.*
   http://ahsri.uow.edu.au
   In the search box, type "exit interview."

3.2.3 Modify Plan of Action as Needed

Title Adjusting on the Fly: Revising Objectives During Program Implementation

Objective The student will be able to utilize data collected from learners to revise objectives.

Directions

1. Read the following *scenario*.

   A smokeless tobacco educational program for adolescents is being implemented in a local community. The following objectives were created for the program.

   a. The participant will be able to list the most serious health problems associated with smokeless tobacco use.

   b. The participant will be able to identify the different types of smokeless tobacco products.

   c. The participant will be able to describe the psychological and physiologic addictive process associated with smokeless tobacco use.

   d. The participant will be able to analyze smokeless tobacco advertisements for manipulative messages.

   During the first meeting, a brief assessment was conducted to determine if participants' needs would be met. The assessment revealed participants already knew a great deal about the serious health problems associated with smokeless tobacco use and seemed quite familiar with types of products available. The results of the assessment further revealed that the participants were very interested in laws concerning tobacco access by minors and smokeless tobacco cessation techniques.

2. In **Table 3.2.3-1**, explain how altering an existing objective, adding new objectives, or deleting objectives from the current list could better meet the needs of the participants.

Student Resource

The Centers for Disease Control and Prevention website has information about smokeless tobacco.

http://www.cdc.gov

In the search box, type "smokeless tobacco."

Table 3.2.3-1 Revising Objectives to Meet Program Participants' Needs

Modes of Improving Original Objectives	Explanation of Needed Improvements in Specific Objectives
Altering an existing objective	
Adding new objective(s)	
Deleting original objective(s)	

3.2.4 Monitor Use of Resources

Title Midyear Budget Report

Objective The student will be able to complete a simple grant budget report sheet.

Directions

1. Review the grant budget sheet in **Table 3.2.4-1**. This is a simple budget for a 1-year diabetes awareness program for African American senior citizens. The grant requires the grantee to monitor the financial resources during the course of the grant.
2. Read the grant summary, keeping in mind that the grant is at the halfway point (6 months of a 12-month grant).

Table 3.2.4-1 Grant Budget Sheet

Line Item	Specific Information	Income from Grant	Expense to Date	Balance
Personnel	Project director	$45,000		
	Administrative assistant	$22,000		
	Student interns Fall Spring	 $1,500 $1,500		
Travel	Conference for staff: 2 nights lodging/2 rooms @ $120 each	$480		
Contractual	Registered dietician: 10 sessions @ $100 per session	$1,000		
	Publicity: Flyers, newspaper ads, posters	$500		
Equipment	20 glucose monitors @ $100 each	$2,000		
Commodities	Wellness packets: 20 at $20 each	$400		
	Program completion T-shirts: 20 @ $10 each	$200		
	Total	$74,580		

Grant Summary

At the halfway point of the grant, the 20 participants have participated in 10 of the scheduled 20 sessions and met with the registered dietitian 5 times. The staff (project director, administrative assistant, and the fall intern) attended the diabetes education conference. Each participant has received and been instructed in the use of the home blood glucose monitors. Each participant has also received a wellness packet.

3. Use the information in the narrative *Grant Summary* in **Step 2** to complete the **Expense to Date** and **Balance** columns in **Table 3.2.4-1**. The total balance has been supplied to assist with the needed resources.

Student Resources

1. Grants.gov
http://www.grants.gov

2. The National Institutes of Health, Office of Extramural Research
http://grants.nih.gov/grants/oer.htm

3.2.5 Monitor Compliance with Legal and Ethical Principles

Title Human Subjects in Research Training

Objective The student will be able to complete official human subjects training.

Directions
1. Use **Student Resources** to find and complete training on human subjects.
2. Write the source of the training and scores received. If available, scan the certificate of completion or any document of proof of completion.

Training source:

Scores:

Student Resources
1. Collaborative Institutional Training Initiative (CITI)
   www.citiprogram.org
2. National Institutes of Health (NIH), Office of Extramural Research Protecting Human Research Subjects
   http://phrp.nihtraining.com
3. Health Resources and Services Administrations, Human Subjects Research
   http://www.hrsa.gov

COMPETENCY 3.3 TRAIN INDIVIDUALS INVOLVED IN IMPLEMENTATION OF HEALTH EDUCATION

3.3.1 Select Training Participants Needed for Implementation

Title Characteristics to Consider When Selecting Individuals to Deliver Training

Objective The student will be able to identify the characteristics to consider when selecting individuals to deliver training.

Directions

1. Find a local American Red Cross Organization and arrange for a 30-minute interview with the health and safety coordinator, or the person charged with selecting individuals to deliver training, to discuss various aspects of selecting individuals to deliver the community first aid and safety course.
2. Use the questions in **Table 3.3.1-1** to guide the interview, adding questions, if desired. It is helpful to send the interviewee a copy of questions in advance.
3. Within 3 days after the interview, send a thank-you note to the interviewee.
4. Use specific examples from the interview to write a one-page summary describing the personal characteristics, personal skills, and organizational context that make the program successful.

Table 3.3.1-1 Interview About Characteristics to Consider When Selecting Individuals to Deliver Training

Name of interviewee:	Job title:
Job responsibilities:	
Educational background/training:	

Interview questions

The following questions pertain to the instructor trainer course that is designed to provide people to teach the community first aid and safety course for the American Red Cross.

Section 1. About the trainer

1. Based on your experiences, what qualities are necessary to be an effective trainer?

2. What problems in communicating to an audience have you seen in some trainers?

3. Does this training require involvement of the audience? Are the materials developed to assist the trainer in getting the audience to participate?

Section 2. About the training materials

4. How long is the training?

5. Are there special technology needs that must be arranged in advance?

6. If a trainer is bilingual, are there opportunities to teach this course in other languages?

7. Are there materials that must be duplicated for audience members? Who does that? Must the trainer be able to duplicate at his/her work or home or does the American Red Cross handle that?

8. Is this training taught by one person or does there need to be a cotrainer?

Table 3.3.1-1 Interview About Characteristics to Consider When Selecting Individuals to Deliver Training *(continued)*

Section 3. About the organization
9. Does this trainer need to obtain or maintain certain certifications to be a trainer for the American Red Cross?
10. Will this trainer need to complete continuing education hours to continue as a trainer?
11. Have trainers been let go or fired? What caused that to happen?
12. What about space? Will the trainer need to be able to provide his/her own transportation to the training site?
13. What other information can be shared concerning recruiting and selecting trainers to represent the American Red Cross?

3.3.5 Demonstrate a Wide Range of Training Strategies

Title The Relationship Between Group Size and Training Strategies

Objective The student will be able to identify a large variety of instructional strategies, including the use of educational media and technology, for training a specific size of a target audience.

Directions

1. Read the following two *scenarios.*

Scenario 1

A school health educator was selected by a state professional health education organization to attend a 1-day workshop delivered by leading experts on conflict resolution for high school students. The school health educator is required to conduct a 2-hour session on conflict resolution as part of regional professional development programs throughout the state during the school year. The school health educator will be conducting education sessions in auditorium settings with over 100 teachers and administrators in attendance.

Scenario 2

A health educator serving as a prevention specialist in a community-based organization received training in inhalant abuse in adolescence. The community health educator is required to conduct professional development programs about adolescent inhalant abuse for school health teachers throughout the state. The community health educator will be providing education sessions at smaller regional settings held in classrooms at local high schools. No more than 25 high school health teachers will be in attendance at each training site.

2. Select one of the two *scenarios* based upon personal interests. Answer the questions concerning instructional strategies found in **Table 3.3.5-1**.

Student Resource

Reading material regarding planning trainings and use of educational media and technology will be provided by the instructor.

Table 3.3.5-1 Comparing Group Size and Training Strategies

Group's size and training strategies: What are the differences?
1. What three instructional strategies would be most appropriate for use with the large group in an auditorium? Why? Provide a citation for a source supporting each selected strategy.
2. What three instructional strategies would be most appropriate for use with small groups in classrooms? Why? Provide a citation for a source supporting each selected strategy.
3. What two educational media and technologies would be most appropriate for use with the large group in the auditorium? Why? Provide a citation of a source supporting each selected strategy.
4. What two education media and technologies would be most appropriate for use with small groups in classrooms? Why? Provide a citation of a source supporting each selected strategy
5. If you were to deliver these training programs, would you select the large or small group? Why?

3.3.6 Deliver Training

Title Deciding the Most Appropriate Method to Instruct an Audience

Objective The student will be able to choose the most appropriate method to deliver training, taking into consideration various constraints.

Directions

1. Complete the activities for **Sub-competency 3.3.5** before completing the activities for this sub-competency.
2. Review the scenarios and information gathered about instructional strategies and technologies from **Sub-competency 3.3.5** and the assumptions about funding and expertise given in **Table 3.3.6-1**. Select *Scenario 1* or *Scenario 2* for this activity and record the choice in the appropriate box in **Table 3.3.6-1**.
3. Below the selected scenario, record a response in each box for the following two questions:
   a. What is the most appropriate method of delivering the training for each of the given assumptions/constraint situations?
   b. What are the reasons for choosing this method?

Student Resource

Completed activities from **Sub-competency 3.3.5**

Table 3.3.6-1 Choosing the Most Appropriate Method to Deliver Training

Selected scenario:	
Assumptions About Available Funds and Level of Expertise of Individuals Providing the Training	**Question Responses**
Extremely limited funding, highly qualified staff to provide the training	a. b.
Extremely limited funding and many entry-level staff members with limited professional experience to provide the training	a. b.
Moderate training funding, but many entry-level staff members with limited professional experience to provide the training	a. b.

(continues)

Table 3.3.6-1 Choosing the Most Appropriate Method to Deliver Training *(continued)*

Moderate training funding and a highly qualified staff to provide the training	a. b.
Unlimited funds, highly qualified staff (in a perfect world)	a. b.

Conduct Evaluation and Research Related to Health Education

INTRODUCTION

This chapter presents 23 activities important to conducting evaluation and research in health education that address 25 entry-level sub-competencies in Area of Responsibility IV.

Students will be introduced to the steps and standards of the Centers for Disease Control and Prevention's Framework for Evaluation, other evaluation models used in health education, the Health Insurance Portability and Accountability Act (HIPAA) Privacy Rule, the *Code of Ethics for the Health Education Profession*, and health impact assessments. Activities include opportunities to explore available databases like the Education Resources Information Center (ERIC) health and psychosocial instrument and national survey tools such as Monitoring the Future and the Behavioral Risk Factor Surveillance System. Students will expand and apply their knowledge of self-selected topics to the development and implementation of a plan for evaluation or research.

Students will practice skills in developing a logical plan for critiquing literature to enable them to present findings from a research literature review. Also, they will be able to identify commonly used data collection instruments, assess the strengths and limitations of qualitative and quantitative data collection methods, and determine validity of such instruments. Students will then be challenged to develop a data analysis plan, conduct data analyses, and interpret and apply findings from evaluation or research.

Students will apply ethical standards to evaluation/research by identifying specific sections of the *Code of Ethics for the Health Education Profession* violated by specific events of the Tuskegee syphilis study and suggest ways the events could have been changed to comply with the code of ethics research and evaluation component. Students will practice data management skills by using spreadsheets and statistical software for coding, entering, and analyzing descriptive statistics for a data collection instrument.

For this text, please go to the student companion website at **go.jblearning.com/PracticalApp** to complete activities using e-templates, and then pass your completed activities to your instructor for review of grading.

COMPETENCY 4.1 DEVELOP EVALUATION/RESEARCH PLAN

4.1.3 Assess Feasibility of Conducting Evaluation/Research

Title Is This Research Feasible?

Objective The student will be able to apply standards to assess the feasibility of a research plan.

Directions

1. The Centers for Disease Control and Prevention has developed a program evaluation framework to assist with program evaluation efforts. One component of the framework identifies standards for assessing the feasibility of conducting research and evaluation. Follow the directions in **Student Resource** to find the feasibility standards to complete this activity.

2. Read the following *scenario* carefully. It describes a plan to evaluate an antibullying curriculum.

   A school district is contemplating the purchase of a comprehensive antibullying curriculum. Before officials make a final decision, they plan to pilot test a component in one of the middle schools. To evaluate the curriculum, a professional evaluation consulting company will be hired. The company's plan for evaluation follows.

   a. *Student satisfaction.* Students will complete teacher evaluations at the end of the program. Teachers with the highest or best evaluations will be given free materials to use in their classrooms.

   b. *Student awareness.* A preprogram and postprogram questionnaire will be administered to students assessing their change in knowledge and awareness of bullying matters.

   c. *Bullying incidents.* School records of bullying incidents prior to the program will be compared to recorded incidents 6 months after program implementation.

   d. *Student interviews.* Extensive interviews will be conducted with all students enrolled in the program concerning their bullying experiences. These interviews will be repeated 5 years after the students graduate from high school.

   e. *Cost.* The program is expected to cost $175,000.

3. Complete **Table 4.1.3-1** to assess the antibullying evaluation plan using the four standards under the group title of "Feasibility" provided in the CDC program evaluation framework.

Table 4.1.3-1 Applying Feasibility Standards to an Antibullying Curriculum Evaluation Plan

Feasibility Standards	Meets Standard		Explain Why the Plan Does or Does Not Meet Each Standard; If It Does Not Meet the Standard, Suggest How It Can Be Changed to Better Meet the Standard
	Yes	No	
1. Realistic			
2. Prudent			
3. Diplomatic			
4. Frugal			

Student Resource

CDC website

http://www.cdc.gov

    a. Find the feasibility standards by entering "CDC Framework Program Evaluation" in the search box.

    b. Find and click "CDC—A Framework for Program Evaluation."

    c. The link provides access to "Standards" located in the left-column menu under "Program Evaluation." Click on "Standards" to find feasibility standards information.

4.1.4 Critique Evaluation and Research Methods and Findings Found in the Related Literature

4.1.5 Synthesize Information Found in the Literature

Title Conducting a Research Literature Search

Objectives

1. The student will be able to follow a developed logical plan for searching research and evaluation literature.
2. The student will be able to present findings from a research literature review.

Directions

1. For this activity, choose either adolescents (ages 10–19) or young adults (ages 20–24) as a target group.
2. Select a topic of interest (e.g., type 2 diabetes, physical activity, tanning beds) for the chosen target group. Use the topic and age group for this activity when requested to do so in the remaining activities in this chapter. To help select a topic and gather sources, consider using ERIC (the URL for ERIC is shown in **Student Resource**).
3. Identify five sources that address research on the selected topic and target group as shown in the following *sample*. Use APA format for sources.

Sample

Target Group: Adolescents

Topic: The arts and prevention

Phillips, K., Simons, S., & Cavanaugh, R. (2010). The impact of adolescent health and arts program. *Journal of Health and Art, 24*(3), 218–224.

Source 1

Source 2

Source 3

Source 4

Source 5

4. Critique each article by applying the following rating scale in **Step 5** to each component question in **Step 6**.
5. Rating scale:

   0 = not available or provided

   1 = meets expectations

   2 = exceeds expectations
6. Questions
   a. *Title*: Does the title adequately reflect the content of the article?
   b. *Purpose of the study*: Is it clearly stated and delineated?
   c. *Research question(s)*: Are specific questions or hypotheses provided?
   d. *Review of the literature*: Is it relevant to the topic and organized?
   e. *Target group*: Is the target group described?
   f. *Research design*: Is a specific research design mentioned and described?
   g. *Instrument*: Is a data-gathering instrument clearly described?
   h. *Data analysis*: Is the data logically described with use of text and tables or charts?
   i. *Conclusions*: Are conclusions unbiased and based upon the results presented?
7. Complete **Table 4.1.4-1** by recording rating results for each article in the appropriate column.
8. Create a slide show (such as PowerPoint) or similar presentation summarizing the findings. Use the questions in **Step 6** to organize the presentation and the rating scale to compare information in the different articles. Provide a ranking of the articles with the highest total scores to those with the lowest scores. Be sure to include a final conclusion or summary of what was learned from the literature search.

Table 4.1.4-1 Rating Scale to Critique Articles in Related Research Literature

Component to Be Rated	Article Sources by Number and Title					
	Sample with Ratings	1	2	3	4	5
Title	2					
Purpose of study	2					
Research questions	1					
Literature review	2					
Target group	2					
Research design	2					
Instrument	2					
Data analysis	2					
Conclusion	1					
Total score	16					

Student Resource

Education Resources Information Center (ERIC)

http://www.eric.ed.gov

In the search box, type in "adolescents" or "young adult." Leave the keywords alone. Click on "Search."

In the "Add Search Criteria," type the topic of interest and click on "Search Again." Number each sentence 1 though 4.

4.1.6 Assess the Merits and Limitations of Qualitative and Quantitative Data Collection for Evaluation

Title Qualitative Versus Quantitative Data Collection

Objective The student will be able to identify the strengths and limitations of qualitative and quantitative data collection methods.

Directions

1. Find four dissertations or theses using the sources in **Student Resources**. Two sources must use a qualitative data collection design and the others a quantitative data collection design.
2. Create a chart that summarizes the differences between the qualitative and quantitative dissertations or theses for the following components:
   a. Purpose of the study
   b. Data collection methods
   c. Type of data collected
   d. Type of analysis
3. Select one of the dissertations or theses used from **Step 1**. Explain why the other research method may not have worked for that particular study. For example, if the study used quantitative methods, explain why a qualitative approach would not meet the purpose of the study.

Student Resources

1. Check the dissertations and theses collection in the school library.
2. Ask a professor to see his/her thesis or dissertation.
3. Many universities have electronic thesis and dissertation websites. Some examples are listed here.
   a. OhioLINKS ETDs (http://etd.ohiolink.edu)
   b. Louisiana State University Electronic Thesis and Dissertation Collection (http://etd.lsu .edu/cgi-bin/ETD-browse/browse)
4. ERIC
   http://www.eric.ed.gov
   a. Use "program evaluation" as a search term.
   b. In the empty space below "Add Search Criteria," enter either the term "quantitative" or "qualitative" and click "Search."
   c. One more time, below "Add Search Criteria," enter "dissertations and theses."

4.1.8 Identify Existing Data Collection Instruments

Title Data Collection Instruments in Health Education

Objective The student will be able to identify major data collecting instruments commonly used in the health field.

Directions
1. Use the target group identified for literature search in **Activity 4.1.4** for this activity.
2. Using the resources provided in **Student Resources**, find three different major data collection instruments relating to the target group.
3. Complete **Table 4.1.8-1** by incorporating the following information found in **Step 2** for each of the three instruments:
   a. Title
   b. Purpose of the instrument
   c. Main target group
   d. Method of data collection (e.g., interview, telephone, email)
   e. Types of questions (e.g., multiple choice, open ended, ranking)
   f. Source (who created or administered the instrument?)

Student Resources
1. American College Health Association, National College Health Assessment
   http://www.achancha.org
2. Centers for Disease Control and Prevention, National Center for Health Statistics
   http://www.cdc.gov
   Enter "National Center for Health Statistics" in the search box and select the "National Center for Health Statistics homepage" link. In the left-menu column, click on one of the national surveys.
3. Centers for Disease Control and Prevention, Behavioral Risk Factor Surveillance System
   http://www.cdc.gov
   In the search box, type in "Behavioral Risk Factor Surveillance."

Table 4.1.8-1 Types of Data Collection Instruments

Information Areas	Instrument 1	Instrument 2	Instrument 3
1. Instrument title			
2. Purpose of the instrument			
3. Main target group			
4. Method of collection			
5. Types of questions			
6. Creator or administrator of instrument			

4. Centers for Disease Control and Prevention. Adolescent and School Health
   http://www.cdc.gov
   Use the A–Z Index and locate "Healthy Youth."
5. Monitoring the Future
   http://www.monitoringthefuture.org
6. Partners in Information: Access for the Public Health Workforce
   http://phpartners.org
   In the search box, type "Health Data Tools and Statistics."

4.1.9 Critique Existing Data Collection Instruments for Evaluation

Title Critiquing Data Collection Instruments Used for Evaluation of Quantitative Research

Objective The student will be able to evaluate quantitative research data collection instruments for evaluation purposes.

Directions

1. Use materials provided in **Student Resources** to locate two surveys or instruments that are related to the selected target group and topic in the **Activity 4.1.4** literature search. Do not use national data collection methods found in **Activity 4.1.8**.
2. Compile the information below for each instrument:
   a. Identify the name of the data collection instrument:
   1) Does the title reflect the intent of the instrument?
   Yes   No
   2) Do the questions seem to relate to the purpose of the study?
   Yes   No
   3) Do the questions relate to the target group identified in the title or description?
   Yes   No
   4) Is there any mention of validity or reliability in the description of the instrument?
   Yes   No
   5) Does the length of the instrument seem reasonable? (15 minutes or less)
   Yes   No
   6) Are there expenses involved with the instrument (e.g., copyright costs, costs to purchase)?
   Yes   No
   7) Are there instructions for administering the instrument?
   Yes   No
   8) Is the scoring method described or provided?
   Yes   No
   9) Was the instrument pilot tested?
   Yes   No
   b. Would this instrument be selected to conduct an evaluation of the research study of the selected target group?
   Yes   Yes, with revisions and adaptation   No
   c. Defend response selected in question b by composing a short paragraph. Be sure to be specific with reasons, needed revisions, or adaptations.

Student Resources

1. Databases
   a. HAPI (Health and Psychosocial Instruments)
   b. CINAHL (Cumulative Index to Nursing & Allied Health Literature)
   c. PsycINFO
   d. Mental Measurements Yearbook
   These are searchable databases dealing with health assessment instruments and questionnaires. As these are by subscription only, check the school's library to see availability.
2. ERIC
   http://www.eric.ed.gov
   Use key words such as "questionnaire development" and "health" to narrow the search. If an article does not contain an actual survey, try going to the journal website.
3. Search the theses and dissertations collection in the school's library

4.1.12 Develop Data Analysis Plan for Evaluation

Title Steps in Data Analysis Plan

Objective The student will be able to identify the steps in developing a data analysis plan.

Directions

1. Revisit one of the dissertations or theses used in **Activity 4.1.6**. Review the methods chapter of the dissertation or thesis. In this chapter, typically Chapter 3, the author will provide a description of how the research was done, including elements such as data collection methods, instrumentation, and data analysis.
2. Take note of the procedures described for collecting and analyzing the data.
3. Answer the following questions:
   a. How was the data collected? What methods were used (interviews, surveys, observations, or others)?
   b. Were there any preparation activities described that were needed to plan for the data collection, such as pilot testing the instruments, obtaining institutional review board (IRB) permission, obtaining consent forms, getting approval, or obtaining pretest data or preprogram data?
   c. How was data analyzed? What statistical methods or techniques were mentioned?

Student Resources

1. Thesis Works
   http://thesisworks.com
   Type "methodology" in the search box.
2. An Internet search using the phrase "How to write Chapter 3 Methodology" will be helpful in finding resources to complete this activity.

4.1.14 Apply Ethical Standards in Developing the Evaluation/Research Plan

Title *Code of Ethics for the Health Education Profession* and the Tuskegee Syphilis Study

Objective The student will be able to apply the *Code of Ethics for the Health Education Profession* to the Tuskegee syphilis study.

Directions

1. Go to the Centers for Disease Control and Prevention website (http://www.cdc.gov), type "Tuskegee" into the search box, and click on the Search button. Choose a few articles and read about the Tuskegee syphilis study.
2. Find and review "Article V (Long Version): Responsibility in Research and Evaluation," of the *Code of Ethics for the Health Education Profession* (Coalition of National Health Education Organizations, 2011). See **Student Resources** for help locating the code.
3. Select at least two of the eight sections under "Article V, Responsibility in Research and Evaluation" where the code of ethics was violated in the Tuskegee study.
   a. Identify the section number under Article V and its description that was violated in the Tuskegee syphilis study.

   Section number and description:

   b. Describe the specific event in the study that violated the selected section number in the code of ethics.

   Tuskegee event:

   c. Suggest two ways in which the violation component of the study could have been changed to meet the research and evaluation component of the code of ethics.

   Suggestions for changes:

Student Resources

1. Centers for Disease Control and Prevention
   http://www.cdc.gov
   Type "Tuskegee" into the search box.
2. Society for Public Health Education (SOPHE)
   http://www.sophe.org
   Type "Code of ethics" in the search box. On the Search Results page, select the SOPHE—Society for Health Education Ethics link.
3. The Coalition of National Health Education Organizations. (2011). *Code of ethics for the health education profession* (long version).
   http://www.cnheo.org
   Click on the Code of Ethics—Long version link.

Reference

The Coalition of National Health Education Organizations. (2011). *Code of ethics for the health education profession* (long version). Retrieved from http://www.cnheo.org/PDF%20files/CODE%20OF%20ETHICS%202011%20Full.pdf

COMPETENCY 4.2 DESIGN INSTRUMENTS TO COLLECT EVALUATION/ RESEARCH DATA

4.2.1 Identify Useable Questions from Existing Instruments

4.2.2 Write New Items to Be Used in Data Collection for Evaluation

Title Creating a Survey

Objectives
1. The student will be able to identify useable questions from existing instruments.
2. The student will be able to write questions for data collection.

Directions
1. For this activity, use one of the two surveys located in **Activity 4.1.9**.
2. Review the materials from Creative Research Systems on creating an evaluation instrument. The website address can be found in the **Student Resource**.
3. Evaluate the chosen target group for the chosen topic using a method of evaluation, such as a questionnaire, telephone interview, face-to-face interview, or other method.
4. Choose five questions from the instrument chosen in **Step 1** that can be used to conduct an evaluation of the target group and topic chosen in **Activity 4.1.4**.
5. List these questions in **Table 4.2.1-1**, then address the items listed in the table for each question. These items should be considered when choosing questions for a particular population.
6. Create three additional questions and add them to **Table 4.2.1-1**, and address added items listed in the table for each question.

Table 4.2.1-1 Using Existing Questions and Adding New Ones

Existing and New Questions	How Does This Question Address the Goals of the Evaluation?	Will the Target Audience Understand the Question?	Has Anyone Used This Question with a Similar Target Population?	Identify the Origin of the Question in Order to Give Proper Credit.
1.				
2.				
3.				
4.				

Table 4.2.1-1 Using Existing Questions and Adding New Ones *(continued)*

5.				
6.				
7.				
8.				

Student Resource

Creative Research Systems posts information about survey instrument development.
http://www.surveysystem.com
Enter "survey design" into the search box.

4.2.4 Establish Validity of Data Collection Instruments

Title Understanding Validity

Objective The student will be able to determine the content validity of a questionnaire administered to a target population.

Directions

1. Review the concepts of questionnaire construction provided by the instructor.
2. Describe the following terms: *validity, face validity, content validity, criterion-related validity,* and *construct validity.*
3. Construct a 10-question survey on the topic area chosen in **Activity 4.1.4**. Write it so that it can be administered to college students. Include instructions on how to answer the questions. Closed-ended questions must have two or more responses.
4. In addition, write a paragraph discussing the reasons to ask or not to ask demographic questions in determining the content validity of a questionnaire.
5. Give this questionnaire to two classmates to review and provide feedback as to the reasonableness of the questions for the chosen topic. This establishes face validity. Make changes based on feedback and save the second copy to submit to the instructor.
6. Ask two professors with expertise in this content area to evaluate the questions for content validity using **Table 4.2.4-1**. Make changes to the survey as necessary.

Student Resources

1. Creative Research Systems posts information about survey instrument development.
   http://www.surveysystem.com
   In the search box, enter "survey design."
2. Jack, L., Jr., Hayes, S., Scharalda, J. G., Stetson, B., Jones-Jack, N., Valliere, M., … LeBlanc, C. (2010). Appraising quantitative research in health education: Guidelines for public health educators. *Health Promotion Practice, 11*(2), 161–165.

Table 4.2.4-1 Determining Content Validity of a Questionnaire

Directions: For each question listed, put a check mark in the appropriate box for each of the three options indicated. Please make comments on how to improve the question.					
Question 1:					
Question as Stated		**Clearly Stated**		**Response Options**	
Appropriate for chosen topic	Inappropriate for chosen topic	Yes	No	Adequate number and/or type of response options	Inadequate number and/or type of response options
Comments on question or responses:					
Question 2:					
Question as Stated		**Clearly Stated**		**Response Options**	
Appropriate	Inappropriate	Yes	No	Adequate	Inadequate
Comments on question or responses:					

Table 4.2.4-1 Determining Content Validity of a Questionnaire *(continued)*

Question 3:					
Question as Stated		**Clearly Stated**		**Response Options**	
Appropriate	Inappropriate	Yes	No	Adequate	Inadequate
Comments on question or responses:					

Question 4:					
Question as Stated		**Clearly Stated**		**Response Options**	
Appropriate	Inappropriate	Yes	No	Adequate	Inadequate
Comments on question or responses:					

Question 5:					
Question as Stated		**Clearly Stated**		**Response Options**	
Appropriate	Inappropriate	Yes	No	Adequate	Inadequate
Comments on question or responses:					

Question 6:					
Question as Stated		**Clearly Stated**		**Response Options**	
Appropriate	Inappropriate	Yes	No	Adequate	Inadequate
Comments on question or responses:					

Question 7:					
Question as Stated		**Clearly Stated**		**Response Options**	
Appropriate	Inappropriate	Yes	No	Adequate	Inadequate

(continues)

Table 4.2.4-1 Determining Content Validity of a Questionnaire *(continued)*

Comments on question or responses:					

Question 8:

Question as Stated		Clearly Stated		Response Options	
Appropriate	Inappropriate	Yes	No	Adequate	Inadequate

Comments on question or responses:					

Question 9:

Question as Stated		Clearly Stated		Response Options	
Appropriate	Inappropriate	Yes	No	Adequate	Inadequate

Comments on question or responses:					

Question 10:

Question as Stated		Clearly Stated		Response Options	
Appropriate	Inappropriate	Yes	No	Adequate	Inadequate

Comments on question or responses:					

Reprinted with permission from Greenwalt, T. L. (1998). *The health promotion activities of religious organizations in Delaware County, IN* (Master's thesis). Ball State University, Muncie, IN.

Reference

Greenwalt, T. L. (1998). *The health promotion activities of religious organizations in Delaware County, IN* (Master's thesis). Ball State University, Muncie, IN.

4.2.5 Establish Reliability of Data Collection Instruments

Title Making Sure an Instrument Is Reliable

Objectives
1. The student will be able to describe reliability terms.
2. The student will be able to apply measures of reliability.

Directions
1. Complete **Activity 4.2.4**.
2. Review information on reliability provided by the instructor.
3. Use **Table 4.2.5-1** to describe these terms: *reliability, internal consistency, test-retest reliability, rater reliability*, and *parallel forms reliability*.
4. Use the survey that was constructed in **Activity 4.2.4**. Administer the survey to 10 college students. Wait 2 weeks, and then repeat the survey to the same students.
5. Check the test-retest reliability of the survey by using **Table 4.2.5-2** to compare the results of both surveys for each of the 10 people.
6. Revise problematic questions to produce more consistency if inconsistencies exist.

Table 4.2.5-1 Describing Reliability

Term to Describe	Description
Reliability	
Internal consistency	
Test-retest reliability	
Rater reliability	
Parallel forms reliability	

Table 4.2.5-2 Determining Test-Retest Reliability for a Questionnaire

Question Number	Were the Responses Similar Between the First and Second Administration? Yes or No	Were the Responses Different Between the First and Second Administration? Yes or No	Comments About Similarities/Differences for Each Question
1.			
2.			

(continues)

Table 4.2.5-2 Determining Test-Retest Reliability for a Questionnaire *(continued)*

3.			
4.			
5.			
6.			
7.			
8.			
9.			
10.			

Student Resources
1. Material is provided by instructor on reliability.
2. Centers for Disease Control and Prevention
   http://www.cdc.gov
   In the search box, type "Test-retest reliability" for journal articles related to this topic.

COMPETENCY 4.3 COLLECT AND ANALYZE EVALUATION/RESEARCH DATA

4.3.1 Collect Data Based on the Evaluation/Research Plan

Title Evaluation Models and Frameworks for the Development of an Evaluation Plan

Objectives

1. The student will be able to apply an evaluation model used in health education to an evaluation plan.
2. The student will be able to summarize the CDC evaluation framework.

Directions

1. Review the material provided by the instructor pertaining to the evaluation models used in health education: attainment model, decision-making model, goal-free model, naturalistic model, systems analysis model, and utilization-focused model.
2. For this activity, review the surveys or instruments in **Activity 4.1.9** and the survey developed in **Activity 4.2.4**.
3. Which one of the models referred to in **Step 1** best fits the survey evaluated in **Activity 4.1.9**? Why does this model fit the best? Describe the model and the characteristics of the survey that fit it.
4. Which one of the models referred to in **Step 1** best fits the survey created in **Activity 4.2.4**? Why does this model fit the best? Describe the model and the characteristics of the survey that fit it.
5. Review the *CDC Framework for Program Evaluation* that can be found at http://www.cdc .gov/healthyyouth/evaluation/resources.htm.
6. Read the article about evaluating the program entitled, "Alive!" and then respond to the questions found in **Table 4.3.1-1**. The full reference can be found in the **Student Resources**.

Table 4.3.1-1 Applying the CDC Six-Step Framework for Program Evaluation to the Alive! Program

Questions About Steps in Evaluation Practice	Responses
1. *Engage stakeholders.* Who was involved in the program's development? Who were the primary intended users?	
2. *Describe the program.* What was the need for the program? What was the expected effect? What activities were involved? What resources did the implementers have at their disposal? Did they provide a logic model?	
3. *Focus the evaluation design.* What was the purpose of evaluating this program? Did the implementers provide the questions that were asked? What method was used to evaluate the program?	
4. *Gather credible evidence.* What data was gathered? Was it adequate to address the effectiveness of the Alive! program?	

(continues)

Table 4.3.1-1 Applying the CDC Six-Step Framework for Program Evaluation to the Alive! Program *(continued)*

	Responses
5. *Justify conclusions.* What statistical program was used to analyze the data? Did the implementers' interpretation fit the data they gathered? What recommendations came from this study?	
6. *Ensure use and share lessons learned.* Does it suffice to publish this as a way of sharing the implementers' lessons? Did they make any changes to the Alive! Program based on their findings? Would one be able to implement this program in one's community based on this study?	
Questions About Standards for Effective Evaluation	**Responses**
1. *Utility.* What was the purpose of the evaluation? Who could use the evaluation results and how could they use them?	
2. *Feasibility.* What was the program's stage of development? How intense was the program? How measurable were the components in the proposed focus?	
3. *Propriety.* Did the focus and design of the evaluation adequately detect any unintended consequences? Did the focus and design include examination of the experience of those who are affected by the program?	
4. *Accuracy.* Was the focus broad enough to detect success or failure of the program? Was the design the right one to respond to the questions—such as attribution—that are being asked by stakeholders?	

Adapted from U.S. Department of Health and Human Services. Centers for Disease Control and Prevention. Office of the Director, Office of Strategy and Innovation. (2005). *Introduction to program evaluation for public health programs: A self-study guide.* Atlanta, GA: Centers for Disease Control and Prevention.

Student Resources

1. Centers for Disease Control and Prevention. Office of the Associate Director for Program
http://www.cdc.gov
In the search box, type "program evaluation framework" and select the result for "A Framework for Programs Evaluation." There are links to numerous materials on program evaluation in the left-column menu.

2. Get Smart Program

 http://www.cdc.gov

 a. Type "get smart" in the search box and select the "Get Smart homepage" result.

 b. Under "Info for Specific Groups," click on "Program Planners."

 c. Scroll down to the Evaluation Manual and download "Step 3: Focus the Evaluation Design."

3. Block, G., Sternfeld, B., Block, C. H., Block, T. J., Norris, J., Hopkins, D., … Clancy, H. A. (2009). *Development of Alive! (a lifestyle intervention via email), and its effect on health-related quality of life, presenteeism, and other behavioral outcomes: Randomized controlled trial.* Originally published in the *Journal of Medical Internet Research* (2008, November 19). http://www.jmir.org

 a. Click on the "2008 (vol. 10)" link in the left-column menu. Scroll down to Number 4 (Oct–Dec).

 b. The article can also be accessed at http://www.ncbi.nlm.nih.gov/pubmed.

 In the search box, type either the title of the article or authors' names.

Reference

U.S. Department of Health and Human Services. Centers for Disease Control and Prevention. Office of the Director, Office of Strategy and Innovation. (2005). *Introduction to program evaluation for public health programs: A self-study guide.* Atlanta, GA: Centers for Disease Control and Prevention.

4.3.2 Monitor Data Collection and Management

Title Creating a Form Summarizing Survey Data

Objective The student will be able to develop a document to prepare survey data for analysis.

Directions
1. Use the surveys that were pilot tested in **Activity 4.2.5**.
2. Assign each individual survey a unique identification number.
3. Develop a code book for the survey. Keep a copy of this code book.
4. Create a new file in SPSS or a similar statistical software program.
5. Define variables in SPSS based on the code book developed in **Step 4**.
6. Enter the data from the survey into SPSS, using the code developed in **Step 4**.

Student Resources
1. Resources provided by the instructor on preparing (managing, coding, and entering) data for analysis
2. Software for conducting statistical analysis, such as SPSS

4.3.3 Analyze Data Using Descriptive Statistics

Title Descriptive Data and Scales of Measurement

Objectives
1. The student will be able to conduct descriptive data analysis.
2. The student will be able to describe scales of measurement.

Directions
1. Complete **Activity 4.3.2**.
2. Analyze the descriptive data for each quantitative (or close-ended) survey question for which data was entered in **Activity 4.3.2**. Use SPSS or other statistical software to produce the following descriptive statistics:
   a. Frequencies (e.g., raw numbers) for all response options
   b. Percentages for all response options
3. Review information on scales of measurement (nominal, ordinal, interval, and ratio) provided by the instructor.
4. Use **Table 4.3.3-1** to describe the general characteristics, give an example of each of the scales of measurement, and indicate which measures of central tendency (mean, median, or mode) can be used with the specific scale of measurement.
5. Identify the scale of measurement (nominal, ordinal, interval, and ratio) for each survey question that was analyzed in **Step 2**.
6. Edit survey questions, if appropriate, and/or add new survey questions to ensure that more questions are written to capture interval and ratio measurements.

Student Resources
1. Resources provided by the instructor on scales of measurement
2. Software for conducting statistical analysis, such as SPSS

Table 4.3.3-1 Describing Scales of Measure

Characteristics	Scales of Measurement			
	Nominal	**Ordinal**	**Interval**	**Ratio**
General properties	Example: Data that cannot be ordered in a hierarchy and are mutually exclusive			
Example	Male and female			
What measures of central tendency can be used? Mean, median, or mode?	Mode			

4.3.4 Analyze Data Using Inferential and/or Other Advanced Statistical Methods

Title Sampling Techniques and Using Inferential Statistics

Objectives

1. The student will be able to distinguish among the different sampling techniques.
2. The student will be able make inferences about central tendency from a sample distribution of a population.

Directions

1. Use the survey instrument that was pilot tested in **Activity 4.2.5** for this activity, and complete **Activities 4.3.2** and **4.3.3** prior to completing this activity.
2. Review statistics and sampling distributions information provided by the instructor.
3. Use **Table 4.3.4-1** to describe the different sampling methods used in research, discussing strengths and weaknesses of each one.
4. Identify the sampling method that was used to do the pilot in **Activity 4.2.5**. Describe how other sampling methods also could have been used.
5. Make inferences about the central tendency of the data that was entered in **Activity 4.3.2** by computing the mean, median, and/or mode, as was identified for each survey question from **Activity 4.3.3**. Use SPSS or other statistical software to conduct this analysis.
6. Write a summary of the results. Attach the software report of the results to this summary.

Student Resources

1. Resources provided by the instructor on inferential statistics and sampling
2. Software for conducting statistical analysis, such as SPSS

Table 4.3.4-1 Sampling Methods

Sampling Methods	Description	Strengths/Weaknesses
Probability sample (random sample)		
Stratified sample		
Nonprobability sample		

4.3.5 Analyze Data Using Qualitative Methods

Title Conducting a Focus Group Discussion

Objectives

1. The student will be able prepare for a focus group discussion.
2. The student will be able to conduct a focus group discussion.

Directions

1. Read the following *scenario*.

   A health educator in a public health agency has been asked by the supervisor to gather information related to cardiovascular health in the local service area. Types of information to find include health behaviors/risk factors, social environment, physical environment, family environment, and services. The health educator decided to conduct a focus group discussion to begin gathering data.

2. Review the four sources provided in the **Student Resources** to help understand the key focus group methodologies to elicit the attitudes, opinions, and ideas from the focus group participants.

3. Develop the following information in preparation for conducting the focus group activity.

   a. An interview guide that describes the scope of the need areas that will be assessed—for example, a list of the issues to be discussed or the questions to be asked of participants.

   b. A description of the number and composition of the focus groups and participants (e.g., how many groups will be assembled and what the individuals who will be invited to the focus group are likely to offer as far as different perspectives, experiences, and ideas relevant to cardiovascular health).

   c. A description of how potential participants will be invited to participate in a focus group.

   d. A description of the place(s) where the focus group will meet.

   e. A letter of informed consent or description of the consent process.

Student Resources

1. Qualitative Research Guidelines Project found on the Robert Wood Johnson Foundation website

   http://www.qualres.org

2. *The Community Tool Box.* Chapter 3, Section 6, "Conducting Focus Groups"

   http://ctb.ku.edu

   Click on the Table of Contents. Scroll to and click on the link for Chapter 3, then click on the link for Section 6.

3. CDC evaluation Briefs 13, Data collection methods for program evaluation: Focus groups, and 19, Analyzing qualitative data for evaluation

   http://www.cdc.gov

   In the search box, type "evaluation briefs" and select the result for "Program Evaluation – Resources." Scroll to access Brief 13 and Brief 19.

4.3.6 Apply Ethical Standards in Collecting and Analyzing Data

Title Program Evaluation or Research and the Health Insurance Portability and Accountability Act (HIPAA) Privacy Rule

Objective The student will be able to understand the legal and ethical issues that affect data sharing with regard to the HIPAA privacy rule.

Directions

1. Read the material suggested in the **Student Resources** and/or read material provided by the course instructor.
2. Provide a response to the questions in **Table 4.3.6-1** about the HIPAA privacy rule and its application to data sharing for program evaluation and research.

Student Resources

1. United States Department of Health and Human Services, National Institutes of Health. (2003). *Protecting personal health information in research: Understanding the HIPAA privacy rule.* http://privacyruleandresearch.nih.gov
   In the search box, enter "protecting personal health."
2. United States Department of Health and Human Services, National Institutes of Health. (2004). *Research repositories, databases, and the HIPAA privacy rule.* http://nih.gov
   Enter "research repositories" in the search box.
3. Centers for Disease Control and Prevention http://www.cdc.gov
   Enter "HIPAA privacy rule and public health" in the search box.

Reference

Centers for Disease Control and Prevention. (2003). HIPAA privacy rule and public health. *Morbidity and Mortality Weekly Report, 52,* 1–12.

Table 4.3.6-1 HIPAA Privacy Rule and Data Sharing for Program Evaluation/Research

Questions to improve understanding of how HIPAA affects data sharing
1. Why should those who are conducting program evaluation/research be aware of the HIPAA privacy rule?
2. What does the HIPAA privacy rule regulate?
3. What is a covered entity?
4. What is protected health information?

Table 4.3.6-1 HIPAA Privacy Rule and Data Sharing for Program Evaluation/Research *(continued)*

5. Researchers are not a covered entity unless they work for a covered entity. However, researchers can use protected health information that is supplied by a covered entity (e.g., national surveillance data, hospital discharge data, insurance claim data). Answer the following questions related to releasing protected health information for research:

   a. What is privacy rule authorization?

   b. What are the core elements that must be included in a privacy rule authorization?

   c. How is authorization different than informed consent?

6. The privacy rule allows covered entities to de-identify data by removing 18 elements that could be used to identify the individual or the individual's relatives, employers, and household members. List the 18 elements.

7. Are de-identified data considered protected health information according to the privacy rule?

8. If it is not feasible for the researcher to use de-identified data and it is not feasible for the researcher to obtain a signed authorization for use of protected health information, what can the researcher request from either an IRB or from a privacy board?

9. If a waiver or alteration of authorization is granted, what documentation must be provided by the researcher?

10. What is a limited data set?

11. What is a data use agreement, and when must it be implemented?

(continues)

Table 4.3.6-1 HIPAA Privacy Rule and Data Sharing for Program Evaluation/Research *(continued)*

12. May a researcher access protected health information from a covered entity when he or she is preparing a research/evaluation protocol? If yes, what assurances must the researcher give to the covered entity providing the information?

Adapted from Centers for Disease Control and Prevention. (2003). HIPAA privacy rule and public health. *Morbidity and Mortality Weekly Report, 52,* 1–12.

COMPETENCY 4.4 INTERPRET RESULTS OF THE EVALUATION/RESEARCH

4.4.1 Compare Results to Evaluation/Research Questions

Title Comparison of Findings to Expected Outcomes

Objective The student will be able to compare original evaluation/research questions to the results of a specific program evaluation or research investigation.

Directions

Note: Activities for **Competency 4.4** should be completed sequentially to maximize student learning.

1. Use the target group and topic identified for literature search in **Activity 4.1.4** for this activity.
2. Locate a peer-reviewed article that focuses on evaluation and/or research by using the resources listed in the **Student Resource**. An appropriate article will follow the standard research publication format of introduction/background, methods, results, and discussion/conclusions.
3. Obtain instructor approval of the article to ensure an appropriate fit for this activity.
4. Compare the original evaluation/research questions to the results of the investigation by providing a response to the items in **Table 4.4.1-1**. The original evaluation/research questions are typically found in the introductory section of the article and may be labeled as purpose statement, objective(s), and/or research question(s). If not located in the introductory section, these questions may be outlined in the methods section.

Student Resource

Databases may be available through the local college/university library such as Academic Search Premier, Cumulative Index to Nursing and Allied Health Literature (CINAHL), Education Resources Information Center (ERIC), and MEDLINE.

Table 4.4.1-1 Comparison of Results to Original Evaluation/Research Questions

Source (in APA format):
List the evaluation/research question(s) from this source (e.g., purpose, objective, hypothesis):
List the major findings for the evaluation/research question(s):
Make a judgment about how well the major findings compare to the original evaluation/research question(s) based on a three-point scale (0 = not well, 1 = adequate, 2 = very well), and in one-sentence justify the judgment.

4.4.2 Compare Results to Other Findings

Title Comparison of Research/Evaluation Findings to Other Findings

Objective The student will be able to compare and contrast research/evaluation findings of the same priority population and/or similar programs.

Directions

Note: Activities for **Competency 4.4** should be completed sequentially to maximize student learning.

1. Complete **Activity 4.4.1** before completing this activity.
2. Use the same peer-reviewed article that was used in the activity for **Activity 4.4.1**. For the purposes of this activity, this article will be called the "original article."
3. Locate at least two other articles on the same target population and topic. These other articles may be referenced within the original article. If other articles are not adequately referenced and/or discussed in the original article, complete a literature search using one or more of the databases listed in **Student Resource**.
4. Compare the evaluation/research findings from the original article to the findings of at least two other similar studies of the same target population and topic by providing a response to items in **Table 4.4.2-1**.

Student Resource

Databases may be available through the local college/university library such as Academic Search Premier, Cumulative Index to Nursing and Allied Health Literature (CINAHL), Education Resources Information Center (ERIC), and MEDLINE.

Table 4.4.2-1 Comparison of Results to Other Findings

Source for Article (in APA Format)	Major Findings Reported in the Article
Original article	
Other article source 1	
Other article source 2	
Which findings are similar to those in the original article?	
Which findings are different from those in the original article?	

4.4.3 Propose Possible Explanations of Findings

Title Critical Assessment of Evaluation/Research Findings

Objective The student will be able to critically assess the findings of an evaluation/research investigation.

Directions
Note: Activities for **Competency 4.4** should be completed sequentially to maximize student learning.
1. Complete **Activities 4.4.1** and **4.4.2** before completing this activity.
2. Use the same peer-reviewed article that was used in **Activity 4.4.1**.
3. Conduct a critical assessment of the findings of the article by providing a response to items in **Table 4.4.3-1**.

Student Resources
Completed **Activities 4.4.1** and **4.4.2**

Table 4.4.3-1 Critical Assessment of Findings of Evaluation/Research Investigation

Source for original article (in APA format):
1. Are the findings clear? If not, what findings are not clear?
2. Are the findings presented with enough detail? If not, what findings need more detail?
3. Are any of the results surprising or unexpected? If so, what was surprising or unexpected?
4. Are any of the results not immediately explainable?   a. If so, do the author(s) offer an alternate explanation? What is the alternate *explanation?*   b. If the authors do not offer an alternate explanation, what might be a possible reason for the unexplained findings?

(continues)

Table 4.4.3-1 Critical Assessment of Findings of Evaluation/Research Investigation
(continued)

5. Rate the merit, worth, or significance of the findings on a quality scale from 0 to 10 (very poor quality to very high quality). The rating is _____.

6. Describe the reason for the rating in two to three sentences. Give specific examples.

4.4.4 Identify Possible Limitations of Findings

Title Identifying Threats to Validity of Research/Evaluation Findings

Objective The student will be able to identify possible limitations of research/evaluation findings.

Directions

Note: Activities for **Competency 4.4** should be completed sequentially to maximize student learning.

1. Complete **Activities 4.4.1** through **4.4.3** before completing this activity.
2. Use the same peer-reviewed article that was used in **Activity 4.4.1**.
3. Review information from the instructor about methodological limitations in research/evaluation investigations.
4. Identify possible limitations of the findings by providing a response to the items in **Table 4.4.4-1**.

Student Resources

1. Utilize **Activities 4.4.1** through **4.4.3**
2. Information is provided from the course instructor about research limitations

Table 4.4.4-1 Limitations of Research/Evaluation Findings

Source for original article (in APA format):
1. Describe how the study participants were selected.
2. Could there have been bias in how the participants were selected? If yes, how likely was this bias? Defend the answer with examples.
3. Could there have been bias in how information was collected from the participants? If yes, how likely was this bias? Defend the answer with examples.
4. Could there have been any of the following threats to validity? If yes, defend the answer with examples. a. Expectancy effect

(continues)

Table 4.4.4-1 Limitations of Research/Evaluation Findings *(continued)*

b. Hawthorne effect

c. History

d. Imitation of treatment

e. Instrumentation

f. Maturation

g. Social desirability

h. Testing

5. Were there variables that affected the results that were not accounted for in the study design (e.g., confounding variables)? If so, list those variables.

6. Was a p-value or a 95% confidence interval reported?

7. Rate the merit, worth, or significance of the findings on a quality scale from 0 to 10 (multiple limitations/poor quality to very few limitations/high quality). The rating is _____.

8. Describe the reason for the rating in two to three sentences. Give specific examples.

4.4.5 Develop Recommendations Based on Results

Title Develop Relevant, Evidence-Based Recommendations

Objective The student will be able to develop recommendations based on results from evaluation or research that are aligned with stakeholder values.

Directions

Note: Activities for **Competency 4.4** should be completed sequentially to maximize student learning.

1. Complete **Activities 4.4.1** through **4.4.4** before completing this activity.
2. Use the same peer-reviewed article that was used in **Activity 4.4.1**.
3. Review the following list of potential audiences to receive evaluation/research recommendations and add other audiences, if applicable:
   a. Advocacy groups
   b. City councils
   c. Contractors
   d. Healthcare providers
   e. Health insurance agencies
   f. Local programs
   g. Parents
   h. Police departments or enforcement agencies
   i. Schools
   j. State health department
   k. State legislators
   l. Workplace owners
   m. Others (please list)
4. Select three audiences that should receive recommendations based on the results of the evaluation/research.
5. Brainstorm several ways each of the three audiences could use the findings of the evaluation/research. Share ideas in **Table 4.4.5-1**.
6. Develop recommendations for each audience based upon findings from evaluation/research by providing a response to items in **Table 4.4.5-1**.

Table 4.4.5-1 Developing Relevant Recommendations Aligned with Stakeholders' Values and Based on Research/Evaluation Findings

Source for original article (in APA format):
Audience 1:
How can this audience use the findings of the evaluation/research? Provide in one sentence several abbreviated brainstorming ideas based upon evaluation/research findings that could be realistic and relevant for use by this audience.   What recommendations could be given to this audience to ensure use of evaluation/research findings? Provide a one-paragraph response citing specific actions and specific findings/evidence from the article.

(continues)

Table 4.4.5-1 Developing Relevant Recommendations Aligned with Stakeholders' Values and Based on Research/Evaluation Findings *(continued)*

Audience 2:
How can this audience use the findings of the evaluation/research? Provide in one sentence several abbreviated brainstorming ideas based upon evaluation/research findings that could be realistic and relevant for use by this audience.
What recommendations could be given to this audience to ensure use of evaluation/research findings? Provide a one-paragraph response citing specific actions and specific findings/evidence from the article.

Audience 3:
How can this audience use the findings of the evaluation/research? Provide in one sentence several abbreviated brainstorming ideas based upon evaluation/research findings that could be realistic and relevant for use by this audience.
What recommendations could be given to this audience to ensure use of evaluation/research findings? Provide a one-paragraph response citing specific actions and specific findings/evidence from the article.

Student Resources

1. Completed **Activities 4.4.1** through **4.4.4**.
2. Information is provided from the course instructor about stakeholder groups and values of stakeholders.

COMPETENCY 4.5 APPLY FINDINGS FROM EVALUATION/RESEARCH

4.5.1 Communicate Findings to Stakeholders

Title User-Friendly Dissemination of Findings

Objective The student will be able to communicate user-friendly findings to stakeholders.

Directions
1. Complete activities for **Competency 4.4** before completing this activity.
2. Use the same peer-reviewed article that was used in the activities for **Competency 4.4**.
3. Identify one of the three potential audiences that were used for **Activity 4.4.5**. This target audience, or stakeholder group, will be the focus of this activity.
4. Write a one-page, single-spaced, executive summary of an evaluation/research report tailored to the selected stakeholder group. Include a concise description of the following items in the executive summary:
   a. Purpose—evaluation/research questions
   b. Methods—procedures, subjects, data-gathering instruments, data analysis
   c. Results—principal findings of the research questions
   d. Conclusions/recommendations—comparison of results to evaluation/research question and other findings, brief explanation of findings, limitations, and recommended actions
5. On page 2, identify two or more formats (e.g., oral presentations, handouts, mailings, wikis, blogs, YouTube videos, organizational newsletters, community forums) that would be the most user-friendly methods of communicating findings to the selected stakeholder group. Next, provide a justification for the selected format(s).

Student Resource
Utilize the complete activities for **Competency 4.4**.

4.5.3 Apply Evaluation Findings in Policy Analysis and Program Development

Title Understanding Health Impact Assessments

Objective The student will be able to describe the major steps in conducting a health impact assessment.

Directions

1. Read the material suggested in the **Student Resources** and/or read material provided by the course instructor about health impact assessments (HIAs).
2. Provide a response to each of the questions in **Table 4.5.3-1**.
3. Access the UCLA Health Impact Assessment Clearinghouse Learning and Information Center website at http://www.hiaguide.org. Click the Completed HIAs tab.
4. Select three completed HIAs and read the information provided about each HIA.
5. Read the example outlining key features of an HIA found in **Table 4.5.3-2**.
6. Identify key features of each of the three selected HIAs by completing **Table 4.5.3-3**. See example in **Table 4.5.3–2**.

Student Resources

1. Centers for Disease Control and Prevention (CDC), Healthy Places, Health Impact Assessment website
   http://www.cdc.gov
   Type "health impact assessment" into the search box.
2. Information is provided from the course instructor about health impact assessments.
3. UCLA Health Impact Assessment Clearinghouse Learning and Information Center website
   http://www.hiaguide.org

Table 4.5.3-1 Health Impact Assessments (HIAs)

Helpful Questions
What is the definition of HIA?
What are the uses of HIAs?
What are the major steps in conducting HIAs?

Table 4.5.3-2 Example of Description of Key Features of Health Impact Assessments

HIA Title, Location, Year, Group: Conducting the HIA	Description of Policy, Program, or Project	Methods Used to Conduct HIA	Scoping: Health Effects, Determinants of Health Affected by the Decision	Assessment: Population Affected and How It Is Affected	Recommendations to Stakeholders	Effect of HIA on the Decisions or Affected Population
Eastern neighborhoods Rezoning and area plans Environmental impact report, San Francisco, 2007, San Francisco Department of Public Health	Area plans and rezoning proposals for neighborhoods	Predictive models of vehicle–pedestrian collisions; health effects associated with change in environment outcomes documented in an environmental impact report	Pedestrian safety, roadway air pollutant emissions; noise-related conflicts about land use	178,000 existing and future neighborhood residents in area of land use conflicts; 20 additional pedestrian collisions per year predicted; respiratory morbidity for new residents, sleep disturbance	Mechanical ventilation to mitigate land use–air quality conflicts; noise mitigation measures; traffic calming; circulation changes and traffic demand reduction	Adopted mitigation measures for air quality and noise impacts; recommendations for pedestrian safety under review

Adapted from Dannenberg, A. L., Bhatia, R., Cole, B. L., Heaton, S. K., Feldman, J. D., & Rutt, C. D. (2008). Use of health impact assessment in the United States: 27 case studies, 1999–2007. *American Journal of Preventive Medicine, 34*(3), 241–256.

Table 4.5.3-3 Describing Key Features of Health Impact Assessments

HIA Title/Name	Description of the Focus of the HIA	Methods used to Conduct the HIA	Scoping: Health Impact or Determinants of Health to be Affected by the Decision	Assessment of How the Population Was/ Is Affected and How Many Are Affected	Recommendations Given to Stakeholders	Effect of the HIA on the Decisions or Affected Population
HIA 1						
HIA 2						
HIA 3						

Administer and Manage Health Education

INTRODUCTION

This chapter acquaints the student with the administrative functions of the entry-level health educator through 18 activities that address 19 of the entry-level sub-competencies in Area of Responsibility V.

Students will examine a systems approach to management, diffusion of innovations theory, major federal laws, regulations and policies pertaining to human resource management (e.g., Americans with Disabilities Act, Family and Medical Leave Act), and the *Code of Ethics for the Health Education Profession*. Many activities are based on case studies or scenarios and will engage students to explore free online management resources. These activities will require students to expand and apply their knowledge of such topics as best practices in professional development, AIDS education and advocacy, increasing physical activity, and emergency preparedness.

Activities will assist students in understanding a systems approach to organizational change and in explaining skills for effective leadership. Students will conduct a SWOT (strengths, weaknesses, opportunities, and threats) analysis and assess an organization's culture. Students will demonstrate how to select, retain, train, and evaluate the performance of volunteers and staff. Students will be challenged with identifying activities that build effective teams.

Students will practice skills in performance evaluation of volunteers/staff by critically analyzing a variety of performance evaluation instruments/tools and selecting an instrument/tool based on a specific job description. Other skills include applying knowledge of characteristics of effective teams to the selection of appropriate team-building exercises and facilitating the development of these characteristics. Students will combine principles of human resource management to evidence-based practice by using information from *Healthy People 2020* and the *Guide to Community Preventive Services*.

For this text, please go to the student companion website at **go.jblearning.com/PracticalApp** to complete activities using e-templates, and then pass your completed activities to your instructor for review of grading.

COMPETENCY 5.2 OBTAIN ACCEPTANCE AND SUPPORT FOR PROGRAMS

5.2.5 Provide Support for Individuals Who Deliver Professional Development Opportunities

Title Best Practices in Professional Development

Objective The student will be able to critique professional development activities using best practice guidelines.

Directions

1. During a professional practice experience, either student teaching or internship, identify opportunities provided for professional development, in-service activities, or continuing education events for the staff. Typically, schools and organizations like hospitals and public health departments will support regular in-service, continuing education, or professional development activities or programs. The instructor can help with identifying the appropriate individuals or offices for contact purposes.

2. Request permission to assist with the development or delivery of one event or follow-up tasks after the delivery. Assisting could include tasks such as creating needs assessment or evaluation surveys, data analysis, developing marketing materials, writing an evaluation summary, registering participants, doing an attendee analysis, creating participant packets, or monitoring sessions.

3. Prior to the event, review the sources in **Student Resources** about professional development to become familiar with best practices in professional development.

4. Before, during, or after involvement with the professional development event, gather information to complete the following checklist.

Checklist for Best Practices in Professional Development

__ A specific person is identified to provide leadership for professional development efforts.
__ Procedures/policies exist for professional development planning.
__ Funding is available to support professional development.
__ Professional development activities are supported and encouraged.
__ Target group needs assessment were conducted.
__ A training plan or design (agenda) was developed.
__ An evaluation plan was created.
__ Materials and equipment were obtained and organized.
__ A specific individual was in charge of logistics (e.g., registration, site selection, AV/technology).
__ A variety of marketing techniques was used.
__ Fundamentals of effective training design and adult learning principles were used in the delivery.
__ The physical environment was conducive to learning.
__ Qualified professional development providers were used.
__ Evaluation materials (instruments, surveys) were identified or developed.
__ Evaluation data were collected.
__ A plan was in place to analyze and interpret the evaluation data.

5. Write a summary of the event that includes a description of the professional development topic or focus, role in the event, and the results of the checklist analysis.

Student Resources

1. National Staff Development Council
   http://www.learningforward.org
   In the left column, click on "standards."

2. Professional development: Learning from the best; A toolkit for schools and districts based on the National Awards Program for Model Professional Development.
   http://www.learningpt.org
   In the search box, type "learning from the best."

5.2.6 Explain How Program Goals Align with Organizational Structure, Mission, and Goals

Title Organization Mission and Goals

Objective The student will be able to link an organization's activities to its mission and goals.

Directions

1. Become familiar with the official website of Eta Sigma Gamma listed in the **Student Resource**.
2. Provide the following information about Eta Sigma Gamma:
   a. Mission statement
   b. Goals
3. For each of the goals, identify an activity, service, resource, or opportunity listed at the website that meets a goal. Explain how the item selected relates to the goal. Use the *example* as a guide.

Example:

Goal: Promoting networking activities among health educators and related professionals.

A joint membership is offered between Eta Sigma Gamma and the American School Health Association. This provides an opportunity for students to become members of another professional organization at a reduced rate. Involvement in more than one professional organization increases networking experiences through conferences, seminars, webinars, and projects.

4. Include a reference for the Eta Sigma Gamma website in APA style or style approved by the instructor.

Student Resource
Eta Sigma Gamma
http://www.etasigmagamma.org

COMPETENCY 5.3 DEMONSTRATE LEADERSHIP

5.3.1 Conduct Strategic Planning

Title SWOT Analysis

Objective The student will be able to conduct a SWOT analysis.

Directions

The preferred target audience for this assignment is an academic unit or department in a university.

1. Locate the mission statement, goal, or objective of the unit. Most units or departments will have this information posted on the website.
2. Find examples of SWOT analyses. See **Student Resources**.
3. Brainstorm questions that can be used to get needed information. Narrow the list to three questions for each component. Questions may address issues such as what the department does well, complaints about the department, trends, or issues (e.g., economics, social change) that might impact the department in a positive or negative way.
4. List the questions next:

Strengths
    Q1
    Q2
    Q3

Weaknesses
    Q1
    Q2
    Q3

Opportunities
    Q1
    Q2
    Q3

Threats
    Q1
    Q2
    Q3

5. Ask selected questions by interviewing students, faculty, and staff about their experiences and then enter responses in **Table 5.3.1-1**. Distinguish who gave each answer by using abbreviations: faculty (f), student (s), staff (stf).
6. Complete **Table 5.3.1-1** with the results.

Student Resources

1. Centers for Disease Control and Prevention
   http://www.cdc.gov
   Type "SWOT" in the search box, click the Search button, and find Do a SWOT Analysis in the Communities for Public Health Resource Kit.
2. An Internet search for SWOT will provide models to follow. Specifically, search for "SWOT analysis of academic programs" to locate examples.

Table 5.3.1-1 SWOT Analysis of Academic Unit/Department

Name of Unit/Department:	
Mission:	
Goal:	
Questions per Component	**Responses** **Faculty Member (f)/Student (s)/Staff (stf)**
Strengths Q1 Q2 Q3	
Weaknesses Q1 Q2 Q3	
Opportunities Q1 Q2 Q3	
Threats Q1 Q2 Q3	

5.3.2 Analyze an Organization's Culture in Relationship to Health Education Goals

Title Determining the Level of a Group's Disaster Preparedness

Objective The student will be able to determine a groups' culture in relationship to emergency preparedness.

Directions

1. For this activity select any accessible small group (e.g., family, roommates, a sorority or fraternity, a church group). Identify the selected group.
2. Choose a quiz provided in **Student Resources** that is appropriate for the selected group. Identify the quiz title and source.
3. Administer the quiz to the selected group.
4. In a paragraph, summarize the findings from the selected group. Based upon the results, is the selected group adequately prepared for a disaster? Is a culture of preparedness evident among the selected group?

Student Resources

1. Baltimore County home page
   http://www.baltimorecountymd.gov
   Type "preparedness quiz" in the search box and click on the Search button.
2. An Internet search using "preparedness quiz" will provide examples of quizzes that will be appropriate for the selected group.

5.3.4 Develop Strategies to Reinforce or Change Organizational Culture to Achieve Health Education Goals

Title Diffusion of Innovations

Objective The student will be able to apply the diffusion of innovations theory to increase emergency preparedness in a group.

Directions

1. Use the sources in **Student Resources** to research the diffusion of innovations theory.
2. The theory suggests five stages involved in adopting a new behavior, idea, or innovation, starting with knowledge or awareness. List the five stages with a brief description of each one following the *sample* for knowledge:
    a. *Knowledge.* An individual is exposed to an idea or behavior but may not have enough knowledge or information to proceed or adopt it.
    b.
    c.
    d.
    e.
3. Refer to **Activity 5.3.2**. Review the results of the analysis.
4. For the knowledge stage only, suggest three strategies specific to the selected group. See the sample provided in 4a.
    a. *Knowledge.* Develop a checklist for what should be included in a basic disaster supply kit.
    b.
    c.
    d.

Student Resources

1. An Internet search using the phrase, "diffusion of innovations theory and stages of the adoption" will provide helpful websites.
2. Roger Clarke's website
   http://www.rogerclarke.com
   In the search box, type "diffusion of innovations."

5.3.5 Comply with Existing Laws and Regulations

Title The Family Educational Rights and Privacy Act (FERPA)

Objective The student will be able to describe the requirements of the Family Educational Rights and Privacy Act (FERPA).

Directions
Use the Department of Education website (see **Student Resource**) to answer the following questions:

a. What is the general intention of the law?

b. What institutions must comply with FERPA?

c. What kind of information can be disclosed by school personnel without written consent from the parent or student?

d. At what age are the rights of FERPA transferred from the parent to the student?

e. What are the exceptions to this? For example, when can a parent obtain information about a student who has reached the minimum age of transference of rights?

Student Resource
U.S. Department of Education "Ed.gov" web page
http://www.ed.gov
In the search box, type "FERPA."

5.3.6 Adhere to Ethical Standards of the Profession

Title Doing the Right Thing

Objective The student will be able to decide what the ethical response should be for a given scenario related that to the *Code of Ethics for the Health Education Profession.*

Directions
1. Read the material suggested in **Student Resource** and/or read material provided by the course instructor.
2. Read the ethical situation *scenario* and answer the questions located in **Table 5.3.6-1**.

Student Resource
Code of Ethics for the Health Education Profession (long version). (2011). Coalition of National Health Education Organizations.
http://www.cnheo.org

Reference
Bensley, R. J., & Brookins-Fisher, J. (2009). *Community health education methods: A practical guide* (3rd ed., pp. 24-26). Sudbury, MA: Jones and Bartlett.

Table 5.3.6-1 Choice Versus Coercion and Intimidation

Scenario

A work site health promotion specialist was speaking about motivational techniques at a state health education conference. Mike and Jill were attending the conference and considered this to be an opportunity to hear about how to motivate employees to develop healthy behaviors. They were serving as consultants to a work site health promotion program in their county and were looking for new ideas to motivate participants. The session was precisely what they needed. They listened with interest to the speaker as she explained motivational techniques used in a smoking cessation program.

One of the techniques was to award a bonus at the end of the year to those who stopped smoking. This would be equal to the difference between the insurance premiums paid by the company for a smoker's health insurance and those for a nonsmoker, which amounted to $200 a year. When asked if bonuses were given for other health-enhancing behavior, such as weight reduction, physical fitness, or substance abuse counseling and treatment, the speaker replied by stating, "insurance companies don't charge an extra premium for health risks."

The speaker explained another motivational technique, which was to have mention of the employee's participation placed in his or her personnel file. This, of course, was with the employee's permission. Although this would not be used for promotion or bonus, it would indicate that the employee cooperated in the company's effort to control health insurance costs.

The third technique was to have managers and supervisors who were smokers voluntarily enroll in the smoking cessation program. Although this was not mandatory, the president and two vice presidents of the company were enrolled in the program and made it known that others were expected to do the same. Even the program's slogan, "From the Top Down: A Smoke-Free Company," was an indication that employees were expected to participate. The speaker said that 80% of the smokers participated, which was attributed to leaders of the company serving as role models.

Jill and Mike began to question the techniques used by the speaker. They had a sense of uneasiness about the motivational methods used. It seemed as if the employees were being coerced to join the program. The following Monday, when talking to Dawn, they concluded that the work site health promotion program's approach to motivation was not in compliance with ethical practice.

Table 5.3.6-1 Choice Versus Coercion and Intimidation *(continued)*

Answer these questions about this ethical situation:

1. Was it fair to give a bonus only to those who smoked?

2. Why would the employer want to have information in a personnel file on an employee's willingness to participate in a smoking cessation program?

3. Is there a subliminal message that one would be expected to participate?

4. Does the impression that employees are expected to take part in a program become a matter of coercion rather than choice?

5. Does anyone really have freedom of choice?

6. What if smokers choose not to participate? Might there be consequences?

7. Is it ethical to influence health decisions based on motivational techniques designed to persuade by questionable rewards and intimidation or coercion?

8. Of the principles of ethics, which are at work here?

9. How does the *Code of Ethics for the Health Education Profession* address this situation? Name the article and section that fits this.

10. What are some solutions to this situation?

11. Should Mike and Jill communicate their concerns to the speaker? Why or why not?

Reprinted with permission from Bensley, R. J., & Brookins-Fisher, J. (2009). *Community health education methods: A practical* guide (3rd ed., pp. 24-26). Sudbury, MA: Jones and Bartlett.

5.3.7 Facilitate Efforts to Achieve Organizational Mission

5.3.9 Facilitate Needed Changes to Organizational Cultures

Title Facilitating Efforts to Achieve an Organization's Mission and Changes in Organizational Cultures

Objectives
1. The student will be able to facilitate the achievement of organizational missions and goals.
2. The student will be able to facilitate changes in organizational cultures by adding a goal on preparing for an emergency.

Directions
1. Review the mission and overarching goals of Healthy People 2020; see the **Student Resources**.
2. Go to http://www.healthypeople.gov, click on the 2020 Topics & Objectives tab, and select Preparedness from the alphabetical list of objectives. Read the information on preparing for an emergency, including the Overview, Objectives, and Interventions & Resources tabs.
3. For the group chosen in **Activity 5.3.2**, review its mission and goals. Do the mission and goals support preparedness? If so, list the goal and describe how it supports preparedness. If not, write a goal to achieve preparedness in this organization.
4. Discuss the mission and goals of Healthy People 2020, describing how they support this organization's need to prepare for an emergency.
5. From the Healthy People 2020 "prepare for an emergency" section found in **Step 2**, indicate what steps found in the Take Action tab that the organization selected in **Activity 5.3.2** has already taken. If no action has been taken, discuss with the organizational leadership the implementation of the goal written in **Step 3**.
6. Review the emergency supply kit checklist available at http://www.ready.gov. Look for the link to "Build a Kit" or type phrase into the search box.
7. Request permission from the group chosen in **Activity 5.3.2** to compare this list to the kit already created. What needs to be added to the existing kit? What needs to be replaced? How much will it cost the group to add or replace materials in the existing kit?
8. If no emergency kit has been created, discuss the possibility of developing one with organizational leaders. For this conversation, prepare a list of the items needed in a new kit and what each item will cost. On this itemized list, indicate how often each item will need to be replaced.

Student Resources
1. Healthy People 2020 website
   http://www.healthypeople.gov
   Click on the tab "About Healthy People."
   Click on the "history and development" tab.
   Scroll down to download the "Healthy People 2020 framework" to review the Vision, Mission, and Overarching Goals.
2. Healthy People 2020 preparedness goals
   http://healthypeople.gov
   Click on "2020 Topics and Objectives."
   Click on "preparedness."

5.3.8 Analyze the Need for a Systems Approach to Change

Title Systems Approach to Change: A Case Study

Objectives
1. The student will be able to understand the systems approach to organizational change.
2. The student will be able to apply systems approach knowledge to a scenario.

Directions
1. Read the *Management Case Study* found in **Table 5.3.8-1**.
2. Answer the questions that follow.
3. Review the systems approach to management provided by the instructor.
4. Apply the systems approach to this scenario. What aspects of this approach fit this scenario?
5. What aspects of the systems approach are missing from this scenario?

Student Resources
1. The Free Management Library
   http://www.managementhelp.org
   In the search box, type "systems thinking."
2. Esther Derby Associates, Inc. blog
   http://www.estherderby.com
   In the search box, type "shifting the pattern."

Reference
Johnson, J. A., & Breckon, D. J. (2007). *Managing health education and promotion programs leadership skills for the 21st century* (pp. 23–24). Sudbury, MA: Jones and Bartlett.

Table 5.3.8-1 Management Case Study

Setting

An AIDS-oriented agency in a midsized metropolitan area was being administered by an AIDS patient with only a modicum of managerial or leadership experience. However, because of the capabilities of its staff fund raiser, the agency raised enough to cover its $250,000 annual budget.

Problem

The fund raiser saw the manager as a person without an adequate vision of what the organization could become. The manager seemed content to maintain service to AIDS patients and their families as the primary focus. The fund raiser saw opportunities for AIDS education and AIDS advocacy in the legislature but was rebuffed by the manager, who stated he did not want the organization to take on more than it could do well. The fund raiser talked to the board chairperson about the opportunities and about the need for leadership rather than mere management.

Alternatives considered

One alternative considered was to establish a board-initiated and board-conducted planning task force. Another was to ask the manager to survey six similar agencies in other metropolitan areas as to their size, budget, program emphases, and so on. The third alternative was to replace the director with someone who had stronger leadership skills.

Actions taken

The board decided to direct the manager to survey six similar agencies and to present a summary of the results to the board. The summary was to be presented at the next board meeting so it could be used by an organizational future task force to be created by the board.

(continues)

Table 5.3.8-1 Management Case Study *(continued)*

Outcome

The survey indicated that most of the six agencies were doing more and that their larger budgets were being covered. The organizational future task force decided that the local community would support an increase in the budget and a wider range of activities. The board subsequently developed an expansion plan and directed the manager to implement it. The manager started the process but concurrently began looking for another position more suited to his skills, finding one in 6 months. The fund raiser was promoted to manager.

Answer the questions about this management case study:

1. Is a bigger organization better? Could other organizations have been formed to do the additional tasks? What advantage is there to having one large organization encompass AIDS patient services, education, and advocacy instead of having three separate organizations perform the necessary activities?

2. Can a manager evolve into a leader? How could such an evolution be achieved?

3. How likely is it that the fund raiser was merely attempting to orchestrate a promotion? How might the manager have responded other than by changing jobs? In what other ways might the board have responded?

Reprinted with permission from Johnson, J. A., & Breckon, D. J. (2007). *Managing health education and promotion programs leadership skills for the 21st century* (pp. 23–24). Sudbury, MA: Jones and Bartlett.

COMPETENCY 5.4 MANAGE HUMAN RESOURCES

5.4.1 Develop Volunteer Opportunities

Title Choosing the Right Volunteer

Objectives

1. The student will be able to describe how a voluntary health agency chooses volunteers.

2. The student will be able to describe how a voluntary health agency retains volunteers.

Directions

1. Read the material suggested in the **Student Resource** and/or read material provided by the course instructor.

2. Choose a local voluntary health agency. Examples include the American Cancer Society, the American Heart Association, American Lung Association, American Red Cross, and many others. Contact the chosen agency and request a 20- to 30-minute interview with the health educator or other employee who is responsible for recruiting and managing volunteers.

3. Use **Table 5.4.1-1** to record the answers to the questions.

Student Resource

The Volunteer Centre Merton website This site contains a step-by-step guide to working with volunteers.

http://wwwvolunteercentremerton.org.uk

Select the tab "information bank."

Download the step-by-step guide.

Table 5.4.1-1 Choosing and Training Volunteers

Agency Name:	**Date of Interview:**
Name of Person Interviewed and Position/Title:	
Purpose or Mission of the Organization:	

Questions

1. What role do volunteers have in your agency?

2. Do you have a job description for volunteers? (If so, request a copy.)

3. In what ways are volunteers recruited?

4. Are volunteers interviewed? What kinds of questions are they asked?

5. What skills do you look for in a volunteer?

6. What tasks do volunteers perform for your agency? What are their responsibilities?

7. What training do the volunteers receive? How long does it last?

8. How are volunteers supervised? Who supervises them?

(continues)

Table 5.4.1-1 Choosing and Training Volunteers (continued)

9. Are volunteers given any performance feedback? Is there an assessment form used? (If so, request a copy.)

10. Are volunteers ever let go? Why would a volunteer be dismissed?

11. In what ways does this agency recognize or reward its volunteers?

12. What reasons do volunteers give for continuing service to this agency?

5.4.2 Demonstrate Leadership Skills in Managing Human Resources

Title Learning about Leadership

Objective The student will be able to explain the skills necessary for effective leadership.

Directions

1. Go to The Free Management Library at http://www.managementhelp.org.
   Click the Leadership (Overview) link to read about leadership as background for the activity. Be sure to read the definitions of leadership and the major theories of leadership.
2. Conduct a literature search to learn about transactional leadership theory and transformational leadership theory.
3. Write a paper comparing (how are they the same) and contrasting (how are they different) the two theories of leadership—transactional leadership theory and transformational leadership theory.
   a. List those skills associated with just one of the leadership theories. Then discuss why these skills may be important to one leadership theory and not the other. Give specific examples of several skills.
   b. Discuss how skills of the two major leadership theories may impact effective leadership of health educators in any work settings, such as community, school (K–12), business/industry, or health care.
   c. Cite sources of information in the body of the paper, with a reference list at the end of the paper.

Student Resource

Free Management Library
http://managementhelp.org
In the search box, type "transactional leadership" and "transformational leadership."

5.4.3 Apply Human Resource Policies Consistent with Relevant Laws and Regulations

Title Understanding Employment Laws and Regulations

Objective The student will be able to describe major federal laws, regulations, and policies that apply to human resource management in all organizations.

Directions

1. Research the following major federal laws, regulations, and/or policies that govern human resources by accessing websites found in **Student Resources**:
   a. Title VII of the Civil Rights Act of 1964
   b. Civil Rights Act of 1991
   c. Age Discrimination in Employment Act
   d. Americans with Disabilities Act of 1990
   e. Rehabilitation Act of 1973
   f. Pregnancy Discrimination Act of 1978
   g. Vietnam Veteran's Readjustment Assistance Act of 1974
   h. Fair Credit Reporting and Disclosure Act
   i. Immigration Reform and Control Act of 1986
   j. Family Medical Leave Act of 1993
   k. Workers Compensation
   l. Fair Labor Standards Act
   m. Employee Retirement Income Security Act of 1974
   n. Consolidated Omnibus Budget Reconciliation Act (COBRA)
   o. Unemployment Compensation
   p. Equal Pay Act of 1963
   q. National Labor Relations Act of 1935
   r. Worker Adjustment and Retraining Notification Act of 1988
   s. The Occupational Safety and Health Act of 1970
   t. Health Insurance Portability and Accountability Act of 1996 (HIPAA)
2. Write a brief (2–3 sentences) summary of each of the aforementioned laws, regulations, and policies describing what each governs or mandates.

Student Resources

1. United States Equal Employment Opportunity Commission
   http://www.eeoc.gov
2. United States Department of Labor
   http://www.dol.gov
3. United States Department of Justice, Americans with Disabilities Act
   http://www.ada.gov
4. United States Citizenship and Immigration Services
   http://www.uscis.gov
5. Federal Trade Commission, Bureau of Consumer Protection, Business Center. (1999) *Using consumer reports: What employers need to know.*
   http://business.ftc.gov
6. National Labor Relations Board
   http://www.nlrb.gov
7. United States Department of Labor, Division of Federal Employees' Compensation, State Workers' Compensation Officials
   http://www.dol.gov/owcp/dfec/regs/compliance/wc.htm

8. United States Department of Labor, Employment and Training Insurance, Unemployment Insurance
   http://workforcesecurity.doleta.gov/unemploy
9. United States Department of Labor, Occupational and Safety and Health Administration
   http://www.osha.gov
10. United States Department of Health and Human Services, Office for Civil Rights, Health Information Privacy
    http://www.hhs.gov/ocr/privacy

5.4.4 Evaluate Qualifications of Staff and Volunteers Needed for Programs

Title Identify and Recommend Instruments for Selecting Qualified Staff/Volunteers

Objectives
1. The student will be able to identify advantages and disadvantages of various instruments that aid managers in selecting appropriate personnel.
2. The student will be able to recommend instruments for selecting staff/volunteers based upon a specific job description.

Directions
1. Access HR-Guide.com (HR-Guide.com, 2011), to locate the section titled, "Selection/Staffing," and research each of the following instruments that may be used by managers to evaluate staff and volunteer qualifications:
   a. Interviews
   b. Personality tests
   c. Cognitive ability tests
   d. Work sample tests
   e. Assessment centers
2. Describe and compare the advantages and disadvantages of each of the instruments listed in **Step 1**. Record responses in **Table 5.4.4-1**.
3. Locate two job postings from one of the links listed in the Health Education and Health Promotion Job Bank Resource Clearinghouse (see **Student Resources** for URL).
4. Recommend at least two instruments from the list in **Step 1** to be used to evaluate staff and volunteer qualifications. Justify the recommendations based upon the description of the position located in **Step 3** and the identified advantages and disadvantages from **Step 2**. Record responses in **Table 5.4.4-2**.

Student Resources
1. HR-Guide.com
   http://www.hr-guide.com
2. The Coalition of National Health Education Organizations, Health Education and Health Promotion Job Bank Resource Clearinghouse
   http://www.cnheo.org

Reference
HR-Guide. (2011). *HR-guide.com*. Retrieved from http://www.hr-guide.com

Table 5.4.4-1 Advantages and Disadvantages of Instruments for Selecting Staff/Volunteers

Type of Instrument	Description	Advantages	Disadvantages
Interviews			
Personality tests			
Cognitive ability tests			
Work sample tests			
Assessment centers			

Table 5.4.4-2 Recommended Instruments for Staff/Volunteer Selection Based on Job Posting

Job posting No. 1
Job title:
Name of organization:
Recommended instrument 1:
Justification for instrument 1:
Recommended instrument 2:
Justification for instrument 2:
Job posting No. 2
Job title:
Name of organization:
Recommended instrument 1:
Justification for instrument 1:
Recommended instrument 2:
Justification for instrument 2:

5.4.5 Recruit Volunteers and Staff

Title Planning the Recruitment Process

Objective The student will be able to plan the process for recruiting volunteers and staff.

Directions

1. Access and read Sections 1 and 2 of Chapter 11 of the *Community Tool Box* (see **Student Resources** for the URL) (KU Work Group, 2011a, 2011b).

2. Read the following *scenario*:

   A health educator at a local public health department provides oversight for an obesity prevention program to increase physical activity of adults of different ages through social support interventions in the community setting, at work sites, and at the university.

   The specific *objectives* are:

   a. Within 1 year of program implementation, to increase minutes spent in physical activity by 20% among targeted citizen groups.

   b. Within 1 year of program implementation, to increase frequency of attending exercise sessions by 15% among targeted citizen groups.

   c. Within 1 year of program implementation, to increase number of blocks walked or flights of stairs climbed daily by 15% among targeted citizen groups.

   d. Within 6 months of program implementation, 80% of program participants will report an improvement in their confidence in their ability to exercise.

   Based on evidence of effectiveness, the intervention selected was building, strengthening, and maintaining social networks that provide supportive relationships for increasing physical activity (CDC, 2011).

   The assignment for the health educator is to recruit volunteers who will set up a buddy system, make contracts with others to complete specified levels of physical activity, or set up walking groups or other groups to provide friendship and support within the community, at work sites, and at the local university.

3. Assume the role of the health educator and the accompanying assignment. Respond to the scenario assignment with responses to the following questions about the recruitment process.

   a. Why is a volunteer position required?

   b. What qualifications should the volunteer possess?

   c. When will the services of a volunteer be required?

   d. Who will be recruiting volunteer(s)?

   e. Where will volunteers be recruited?

   f. What methods will be used to recruit volunteers?

   g. How will you know you have selected the appropriate individual(s) to serve as a volunteer (Adapted from Fottler, Hernandez, & Joiner. (1994). *Strategic management of human resources in health services organizations* (2nd ed., pp. 324–325). Albany, NY: Delmar)?

Student Resources

1. *The Community Tool Box.* Chapter 11, "Recruiting and training volunteers." Section 1, "Developing a plan for involving volunteers."
   http://ctb.ku.edu
   Click on the Table of Contents. Scroll to and click on the link for Chapter 11. Click on the link for Section 1.

2. *The Community Tool Box.* Chapter 11, "Recruiting and training volunteers." Section 2, "Recruiting volunteers."
   http://ctb.ku.edu
   Click on the Table of Contents. Scroll to and click on the link for Chapter 11. Click on the link for Section 2.

References

Centers for Disease Control and Prevention, Epidemiology Analysis Program Office, Office of Surveillance, Epidemiology, and Laboratory Services, The Community Guide Branch.

(2011). Behavioral and social approaches to increase physical activity: social support interventions in community. *Guide to community preventive services*. Retrieved from http://www.thecommunityguide.org

Fottler, M. D., Hernandez, S. R., & Joiner, C. L. (1994). *Strategic management of human resources in health services organizations* (2nd ed., pp. 324–325) Albany, NY: Delmar.

KU Work Group for Community Health and Development. (2011a). Recruiting and training volunteers: Developing a plan for involving volunteers. In: *The community tool box* (Chapter 11, Section 1). Lawrence: University of Kansas. Retrieved from http://ctb.ku.edu/en/tablecontents/section_1106.aspx

KU Work Group for Community Health and Development. (2011b). Recruiting and training volunteers: Recruiting volunteers. In: *The community tool box* (Chapter 11, Section 1). Lawrence: University of Kansas. Retrieved from http://ctb.ku.edu/en/tablecontents/section_1107.aspx

5.4.7 Apply Appropriate Methods for Team Development

Title Building Effective Teams

Objective The student will be able to develop activities that focus on building effective teams.

Directions

1. Identify two team-building exercises using the resources listed in **Student Resources**. The team-building exercises must include activities that foster the development of the following characteristics found in effective teams according to Baker, Menkens, and Porter (2010) in *Managing the Public Health Enterprise*:
   a. *Goal development.* Clearly defined group goals and clearly defined individual tasks
   b. *Effective communication.* Environment in which dialogue is encouraged; introverts are encouraged to give ideas; dominant opinions are held to a minimum; conflict is dealt with openly; accomplishments are celebrated; and members know what to do, how to do it, and how roles fit in the big picture
   c. *Analysis of processes.* Debrief and/or review of logistics, processes, outcomes; analysis of failures; constructive feedback provided
   d. *Build commitment:* Build trust and commitment by creating strong social ties and the sense of a caring family
   e. *Build on member strengths.* Create success by assigning tasks based upon team member strengths and nonstrengths
   f. *Build diverse teams with common interests.* Assist diverse teams to discover common interests; hire people who fit with the values of the team/organization and who work well on teams
2. Provide a description (one for each of the two identified team-building exercises) that includes the following
   a. Steps of the exercise (e.g., how to implement the exercise)
   b. Time required
   c. Materials required
   d. Space required
   e. One paragraph describing how the exercise develops characteristics of effective teams (see **Step 1**).

Student Resources

1. A series of five articles by Brian Cole Miller published in the following issues of *Journal for Quality and Participation*:
   a. Quick activities to improve your team, Fall 2007, *30*(3), pp. 28–32
   b. Buttermilk line, Winter 2007, *30*(4), pp. 29–30
   c. Quick activities to improve your team, Spring 2008, *31*(1), p. 24
   d. Newspaper customs, Summer 2008, *31*(2), pp. 19–32
   e. Secret coach, Fall 2008, *31*(3), pp. 23–27
2. Authenticity Consulting, LLC, Free Management Library
   http://managementhelp.org
   Search for "team building."
3. Workshop Exercises
   http://www.workshopexercises.com
   Search for "team building activities."

Reference

Baker, E. L., Menkens, A. J., & Porter, J. E. (2010). *Managing the public health enterprise* (pp. 17–22). Sudbury, MA: Jones & Bartlett Learning.

5.4.8 Model Professional Practices and Ethical Behavior

Title Ethical Decision Making

Objective The student will be able to make an ethical decision based upon standards from the *Code of Ethics for the Health Education Profession.*

Directions

1. Read the long version of the *Code of Ethics for the Health Education Profession* as published by the Coalition of National Health Education Organizations (2011) available at (http://www .cnheo.org). Also, read the material provided by the course instructor about ethical decision making.
2. Read the ethical situation *scenario* in **Table 5.4.8-1** and then answer the questions located in the table.

Student Resources

1. Coalition of National Health Education Organizations (CNHEO). (2011). *Code of ethics for the health education profession.*
   http://www.cnheo.org
2. Materials provided by the course instructor about ethical decision making.

Reference

Greenberg, J. S. (2001). *The code of ethics for the health education profession: A case study book* (pp. 49–50). Sudbury, MA: Jones and Bartlett.

Table 5.4.8-1 Promised Outcomes or Acceptance of Conditions

Don hated working for other people. As a result, when he graduated from college, he decided to develop his own health education consulting practice. Luckily, several health issues became prominent national concerns just as Don's business was starting up. These national concerns gave impetus to his practice. One of these concerns was smoking, and a national campaign was launched to educate people about the dangers of cigarette smoking. Don developed his own smoking cessation program and marketed it to various businesses. As part of his marketing efforts, Don developed a brochure that described the successes of previous smoking cessation programs he had conducted. The brochure stated in large type:

PROGRAM A: 50% QUIT RATE

PROGRAM B: 60% QUIT RATE

PROGRAM C: 45% QUIT RATE

YOUR PROGRAM CAN HAVE THE SAME RESULTS!!

Don derived these statistics by asking how many of those who completed his program quit smoking. However, if those data were examined more closely, they would show that only 20% of those who began Don's smoking cessation programs completed them; 80% dropped out. In other words, only approximately 10% of those who originally started the program (50% of 20% who completed the program) quit smoking.

Don also developed these statistics at the completion of the program. There is a high recidivism rate in smoking cessation; many who have quit by the end of a smoking cessation program will begin smoking again soon thereafter. Considering this fact, probably fewer than 10% of those who initially enrolled in Don's program were not smoking several months after the program. This might mean that approximately 5% of those who initially enrolled in Don's program had really quit smoking.

Answer these questions about this ethical situation:

1. What ethical issue is raised in this scenario?

2. When there are little data to support health education interventions, is it ethical to withhold that fact from prospective employers or program participants?

(continues)

Table 5.4.8-1 Promised Outcomes or Acceptance of Conditions *(continued)*

3. If a health educator believes there are immeasurable benefits of a health education program, is it ethical to advocate the program based on that belief?

4. If, due to conditions required by employers, a program cannot realistically be expected to meet expectations, is the health educator obligated to state that perception?

5. What if that means the program will not be offered at all and so other potential benefits—even though not the ones originally expected—will, therefore, not accrue?

6. How does the *Code of Ethics for the Health Education Profession* address this situation? Name the relevant article(s) and section(s) that apply to this *scenario*.

7. If you were in this situation, what would you change or do differently to make an ethical decision?

Reprinted with permission from Greenberg, J. S. (2001). *The code of ethics for the health education profession: A case study book* (pp. 49–50). Sudbury, MA: Jones and Bartlett.

5.4.11 Evaluate Performance of Staff and Volunteers

Title Performance Appraisal: Understanding the Process

Objective The student will be able to understand the method(s) of performance appraisal employed by an organization.

Directions

1. Contact a health educator who supervises staff and/or volunteers and who is responsible for conducting formal performance appraisals of staff and/or volunteers. Consult the class instructor for a list of suggested local contacts.
2. Make arrangements for a brief interview (telephone, person-to-person, or via email).
3. Use the interview questions found in **Table 5.4.11-1** as a guide. Add two to three questions.
4. Provide a response to the questions in the table after completing the interview.
5. Send the interviewee a copy of the interview guide a few days before the interview.
6. Within 3 days after the interview, send a thank-you note to the interviewee.

Table 5.4.11-1 Questions for Interview About the Performance Appraisal Process

Name of interviewee:
Job title:
Interview questions   1. Are you responsible for conducting performance appraisals of staff, volunteers, or both staff and volunteers?   2. If you are responsible for evaluating both staff and volunteers, is the process the same or different? If different, explain how the process is different and reply to the following questions representing only one process (either staff or volunteer performance appraisal). Please specify if the following questions represent the performance appraisal process for staff only, volunteers only, or both staff and volunteers.   3. How often is the performance appraisal conducted? Or, at what points in time are the staff/volunteers evaluated?   4. What areas of performance are evaluated? For example, attendance, punctuality, time management, attitude, initiative, communication, dependability, adaptability/flexibility, perception/judgment?   5. What steps are involved in the performance appraisal process? Describe the steps taken during the following phases of the process: a. Preappraisal and preparation   b. During the evaluation   c. Closing the evaluation and follow-up   6. What methods are used for providing communication/feedback to the staff/volunteer regarding the performance appraisal?   7. What is the role of the staff/volunteer during the performance appraisal process?   8. Are staff/volunteers given an opportunity and/or required to conduct a self-evaluation of her/his performance?   9. Do you have a process for handling employee behaviors if they become defensive, make excuses, become angry, and/or unresponsive?

(continues)

Table 5.4.11-1 Questions for Interview About the Performance Appraisal Process *(continued)*

10. Does your organization have a formal policy governing the conduct of the performance appraisal process?

11. Did you have formal training on how to conduct performance appraisals? If so, please describe the training.

12. What advice can you give me about the conduct of performance appraisals for staff/volunteers?

13. Other questions:

COMPETENCY 5.5 FACILITATE PARTNERSHIPS IN SUPPORT OF HEALTH EDUCATION

5.5.3 Facilitate Partner Relationship(s)

Title Identify Partners and Establish Relationships

Objectives
1. The student will be able to identify key partners from various organizations who can contribute to developing future programs.
2. The student will be able to facilitate relationships among partners to achieve common program goals.

Directions
1. Access and read Chapter 7 of *The Community Tool Box* (see **Student Resource** for the URL) (KU Work Group, 2011).
2. Read the following *scenario*:

   A health educator at a local public health department provides oversight for an obesity prevention program to increase physical activity of adults of different ages through social support interventions in the community setting, at work sites, and at the university.

   The specific *objectives* are:
   a. Within 1 year of program implementation, to increase minutes spent in physical activity by 20% among targeted citizen groups.
   b. Within 1 year of program implementation, to increase frequency of attending exercise sessions by 15% among targeted citizen groups.
   c. Within 1 year of program implementation, to increase number of blocks walked or flights of stairs climbed daily by 15% among targeted citizen groups.
   d. Within 6 months of program implementation, 80% of program participants will report an improvement in their confidence in their ability to exercise.

   Based on evidence of effectiveness, the intervention selected was building, strengthening, and maintaining social networks that provide supportive relationships for increasing physical activity (CDC, 2011).

   The assignment for the health educator is to recruit volunteers who will set up a buddy system, make contracts with others to complete specified levels of physical activity, or set up walking groups or other groups to provide friendship and support within the community, at work sites, and at the local university.
3. Assume the role of the health educator and the accompanying assignment. Respond to the scenario assignment by preparing a response to the following items, which address methods for identifying partners and establishing relationships necessary to complete the assignment (Fallon & Zgodzinski, 2012):
   a. Identify a list of key partners or stakeholders from various organizations who have the ability to make decisions in support of the program's specific objectives.
   b. For each partner, identify common interests, where coordination is required or beneficial, and where various resources can be used in support of the program's specific objectives.
   c. Prepare an agenda for a meeting of key partners and craft an invitation (either via email or snail mail) to be sent to key partners inviting them to the meeting. If necessary, tailor the letter to specific partners. The agenda should include a process for identifying common interests, specific tasks, and development of formal agreements pertaining to the program's specific objectives.

Student Resource
The Community Toolbox. Chapter 7, "Encouraging involvement in community work."
http://ctb.ku.edu
Click on the Table of Contents. Scroll to and click on the link for Chapter 7.

References

Centers for Disease Control and Prevention, Epidemiology Analysis Program Office, Office of Surveillance, Epidemiology, and Laboratory Services, The Community Guide Branch. (2011). *Guide to community preventive services*. Behavioral and social approaches to increase physical activity: Social support interventions in community. Retrieved from http://www.thecommunityguide.org

Fallon, L. F., & Zgodzinski, E. J. (2012). *Essentials of public health management* (3rd ed., pp. 324–325). Burlington, MA: Jones & Bartlett Learning.

KU Work Group for Community Health and Development. (2011). Encouraging involvement in community work. In: *The community tool box* (Chapter 7). Lawrence: University of Kansas. Retrieved from http://ctb.ku.edu/en/tablecontents/chapter_1006.aspx

Serve as a Health Education Resource Person

INTRODUCTION

This chapter reviews activities for a health educator who serves as a resource person through 12 activities that address 12 entry-level sub-competencies in Area of Responsibility VI.

Students will be guided through activities that will help them to determine what information resources are needed, how to identify valid information sources, and how to critique accuracy of resources. Students will be instructed to use information to develop educational sessions after identifying priority populations and important stakeholders in those groups. These activities will require students to expand their knowledge on topics including cardiac rehabilitation, the *Dietary Guidelines for Americans*, methamphetamines, bullying in schools, and cancer.

Activities will assist students in determining if consultative relationships are appropriate, ranking the consulting components according to skills, defining the role of a consultant, and identifying the scope of work for a consultant. Collaborating with partners and ethical principles in consultative relationships will also be addressed.

Students will evaluate health information on the Internet, use the *Dietary Guidelines for Americans* to provide information, check literacy level of materials developed, identify key stakeholders in creating and maintaining a coalition or partnership, and prioritize who is most important in a school health setting to conduct training on preventing bullying. They will be asked to use a variety of technologies such as PowerPoint to complete some of the activities. Students will review the *Code of Ethics for the Health Education Profession* and apply that code of ethics to a scenario about consulting relationships.

For this text, please go to the student companion website at **go.jblearning.com/PracticalApp** to complete activities using e-templates, and then pass your completed activities to your instructor for review or grading.

COMPETENCY 6.1 OBTAIN AND DISSEMINATE HEALTH-RELATED INFORMATION

6.1.1 Assess Information Needs

Title Choosing Information for Cardiac Rehabilitation Education

Objective The student will be able to assess what information is needed by patients in a cardiac rehabilitation education program.

Directions

1. Read the following *scenario:*

   A local hospital is developing a series of four classes for people who have had a heart attack and are in a cardiac rehabilitation program. The classes will include information on low-fat diets, exercise, reducing risk factors such as smoking and drinking, and other topics. At the end of each class, the patients will go home with handouts and URLs to websites that they can use. The health educator will select materials to serve as handouts plus recommend credible websites to the patients.

2. Using **Table 6.1.1-1**, list one printed source of information and one website for each topic that patients should have at their disposal. For printed materials, indicate the source of the material and where it can be downloaded, if it is online. For websites, identify credible sources with current, relevant information. The two entries across from the Heart Healthy Diet are examples of a helpful, printed material and a website that can be used.

Student Resources

1. American Heart Association
   http://www.heart.org/HEARTORG
2. Health Finder—a government site that lists reputable websites for health topics
   http://www.healthfinder.gov

Table 6.1.1-1 Informational Topics Needed for a Cardiac Rehab Education Program

Informational Topic	Printed Informational Materials with Source	Web URLS with Information
1. Heart Healthy Diet	Mayo Clinic has menus for heart-healthy eating to cut the fat and salt. http://mayoclinic.com	Mayo Clinic has a website that explains a heart-healthy diet. http://www.mayoclinic.com
2. Recipes for a heart-healthy diet		
3. Importance of exercise		
4. List of physical activities that are heart healthy		

Table 6.1.1-1 Informational Topics Needed for a Cardiac Rehab Education Program *(continued)*

5. Importance of quitting smoking and resources for doing so		
6. Information on reducing the use of alcohol		

6.1.2 Identify Valid Information Resources

Title Valid Sources of Information

Objective The student will be able to identify valid health information resources.

Directions

1. Read the following *scenario*:
   The *Dietary Guidelines for Americans* are updated every 5 years. The health educator working in worksite wellness at a national computer company is given the responsibility to keep the nutrition library up to date for employees and their families.
2. Find five valid sources of information for the most recent update of the *Dietary Guidelines for Americans*. Select different types of resources such as a research article, government publication, nutrition-oriented websites, or lay literature.
3. Record findings of valid information resources in the most appropriate columns in **Table 6.1.2-1**.
4. Explain why this information resource is valid. An example has been provided.

Student Resources

1. U.S. Dietary Guidelines Report
   http://www.health.gov
   Click on Dietary Guidelines.
2. Health Finder, a government site that lists reputable websites for health topics
   http://www.healthfinder.gov
   Use Health A to Z to find child, liquid, and maternal nutrition information.
3. Choose My Plate
   http://www.choosemyplate.gov

Table 6.1.2-1 *Dietary Guidelines for Americans:* **Information Resources**

Information Resource	Source of Information	Year Last Updated	Why Resource Is Valid	Web Address Where Information Can Be Found
1. Choose My Plate (replaces the food guide pyramid)	United States Department of Agriculture	2011	Agency that shares information supported by years of reviewing research	http://www .choosemyplate. gov
2.				
3.				
4.				
5.				
6.				

6.1.3 Critique Resource Materials for Accuracy, Relevance, and Timeliness

Title Critiquing Information on the Internet

Objective The student will be able to evaluate health information found on the Internet using the National Cancer Institute Evaluation Tool.

Directions

1. Read the document entitled *Evaluating Health Information on the Internet*. See the **Student Resources** for information on finding this document.
2. Choose two websites that provide health-related information. They can be websites that were found in **Activity 6.1.1** or **Activity 6.1.2**. However, the National Cancer Institute website cannot be evaluated for this activity.
3. Using **Table 6.1.3-1**, answer the questions for each of the two websites selected in **Step 2**.

Student Resources

1. The American Cancer Society, which has a link to evaluating resources
   http://www.cancer.org
2. Health Finder—a site that lists health topics
   http://www.healthfinder.gov
3. *Evaluating health information on the Internet*
   http://www.cancer.gov
   Type, "evaluating health information on the internet" in the search box and click on the Search button.

Reference

National Cancer Institute (NCI). (2011). *National Cancer Institute fact sheet: Evaluating health information on the Internet*. Retrieved from http://www.cancer.gov/cancertopics/factsheet/ Information/internet

Table 6.1.3-1 Evaluating Information on the Internet

Questions	First Health Information Website	Second Health Information Website
1. What is the web address for this information site?		
2. What is the health topic this website addresses?		
3. Who runs the website?		
4. Who pays for the website?		
5. What is the purpose of the website?		
6. What is the original source of the information on the website?		

(continues)

Table 6.1.3-1 Evaluating Information on the Internet *(continued)*

7. How is the information on the website documented?		
8. How is the information reviewed before it is posted on the website?		
9. How current is the information on the website?		
10. How does the website choose links to other sites?		
11. What information about users does the website collect, and why?		
12. How does the website manage interactions with users?		
13. How can people verify the accuracy of information they receive via email?		
14. Where can people find information about health claims found on the Internet?		

Adapted from National Cancer Institute (NCI). (2011). *National Cancer Institute fact sheet: Evaluating health information on the Internet.* Retrieved from http://www.cancer.gov/cancertopics/factsheet/Information/internet

6.1.4 Convey Health-Related Information to Priority Populations

Title National Dietary Guidelines Presentation

Objective The student will be able to develop an educational session on the current *Dietary Guidelines for Americans* for a specific target population.

Directions

1. Choose the intended audience for an educational session on the current *Dietary Guidelines for Americans*. Indicate their range of age, ethnicities, and level of health literacy.
2. Develop a PowerPoint or similar presentation that focuses on current *Dietary Guidelines for Americans* and Choose My Plate materials. Refer to **Activity 6.1.2** for resources and Internet sites with content helpful to the presentation.
3. Integrate within the presentation audience participation that helps demonstrate the concepts related to Choose My Plate found at http://choosemyplate.gov.
4. Test the literacy level of the PowerPoint text for acceptability to the reading level of the audience chosen. Adjust the level of reading if needed. See **Student Resources** for more information on testing readability.
5. Develop a handout explaining how participants can use the Choose My Plate website when at home. Check for the appropriate literacy level and language for the population chosen in **Step 1**.

Student Resources

1. U.S. Dietary Guidelines Report
   http://www.health.gov
   Click on Dietary Guidelines.
2. Health Finder, a government site with links to reputable websites for health topics
   http://www.healthfinder.gov
3. Choose My Plate
   http://www.choosemyplate.gov
4. An Internet search using the phrase "SMOG readability formula" will provide useful resources for this activity.

6.1.5 Convey Health-Related Information to Key Stakeholders

Title Methamphetamine Presentation for Key Stakeholders

Objective The student will be able to design a professional presentation for stakeholders.

Directions

1. Consider the following *scenario*.

   As a health educator in the community, interest is increasing in raising awareness concerning methamphetamine use and eventually creating a task force to address the issue. The first phase of the plan is to identify key stakeholders in the community and present information about the effects of methamphetamine on the individual, family, and society; trends and patterns of use; prevention and treatment efforts; and model programs that have worked in similar communities.

2. The key stakeholders identified included individuals who have expertise in drugs and drug education; members of law enforcement; individuals who have been affected by meth use; concerned individuals for the health and economic well-being of the community; and people involved with community funding and policy making.

3. Design a presentation to communicate the suggested information to the stakeholders (effects of methamphetamine on the individual, family, and society; trends and patterns of use; prevention and treatment efforts; and model programs that have worked in similar communities). The presentation can be in the form of an oral presentation with PowerPoint or similar format, a script for a webinar or video conference, a short report with graphs or tables, or a fact sheet.

4. Use the information provided in **Student Resources**.

Student Resources

1. National Institutes of Health
   http://www.drugabuse.gov
   Click on "drugs of abuse."

2. White House Office of National Drug Control Policy
   http://whitehouse.gov
   In the search box, type "methamphetamine."

3. Drug Enforcement Agency
   http://www.justice.gov
   Click on "DEA drug information."

COMPETENCY 6.2 PROVIDE TRAINING

6.2.3 Identify Priority Populations

Title Who Should Be Trained?

Objective The student will be able to select priority populations for training.

Directions

The following excerpt is from a report titled, *Perception and Practices Regarding School Bullying*, that was written by a committee from a local school system after collecting data about bullying in their school:

> School is where most bullying occurs. In this study most students (over 80%) reported that bullying happened in their school at least sometimes. Most bullying occurs where adults cannot or will not intervene. Bullies take advantage of weak teachers in the classroom and lax supervision or lack of supervision in the cafeteria, on the playground or in school corridors. The principals in this study reported that hallways and on the playground are where most school personnel observe bullying activities. Bullying most commonly occurs in areas where there is little or no supervision. (Used with permission, Dr. Bobbi Mattingly, Regional Superintendent of Schools, Regional Office of Education No. 11, 730 7th St, Charleston, IL)

The local school system committee was able to acquire some funding for bully prevention training. However, the funding is limited and will support training for a limited number of personnel.

1. Assume the role of the health educator on the committee. Suppose you have been selected to identify the priority population to receive the training.
2. Select three of the following groups to attend the training. Based upon the aforementioned *Perception and Practices Regarding School Bullying* report, place an *x* next to the three groups identified to receive the training.
   __ Bus drivers and bus aides
   __ Cafeteria workers
   __ Teachers
   __ Coaches
   __ Office support staff
   __ Administrators
   __ Janitorial staff
   __ Students
   __ Parents
   __ Playground and hallway monitors
3. When prioritizing groups to train within an organization, such as a school system, one factor to consider is who would benefit the most from the training. Specifically, which group would be able to have the greatest impact on the organization after receiving the training? Explain what this means. Use the bully example to support the response.

Student Resource
International Bullying Prevention Association
http://www.stopbullyingworld.org

Reference
Mattingly, B. (2008). *Principals' perception and practices regarding school bullying.* Unpublished report. Charleston, IL: Regional Office of Education No. 1.

COMPETENCY 6.3 SERVE AS A HEALTH EDUCATION CONSULTANT

6.3.1 Assess Needs for Assistance

Title Should I Be the Consultant?

Objective The student will be able to list questions needed to determine if a consultative relationship is appropriate.

Directions

1. Read the following *scenario.*

   An email message was received from an administrator of the local school system. All it said was, "We would like to hire you as a consultant to implement a suicide prevention plan in our schools. Please get back to me as soon as you can with your response." Before the recipient of the email agrees to do the presentation and accept the position as a consultant, more information needs to be gathered about the situation.

2. Working with the instructor, create a list of questions that could generate enough information to allow an informed decision to be made.

3. Once the listed is created, compose an email to the administrator with the questions that need to be answered before one might make a decision concerning such a consulting relationship. These questions will be used again in **Activity 6.3.2**.

Student Resource

The Association of Consultants to Nonprofits

http://www.acnconsult.org

Click on "Find a consultant" to access resources that may help in completion of this activity.

6.3.2 Prioritize Requests for Assistance

Title Consulting Considerations

Objective The student will be able to rank consulting components according to personal skills and preferences.

Directions

1. To complete this activity, use the list of questions created for **Activity 6.3.1**.
2. List the questions first with sufficient space on the right margin to rank each question.
3. Rank the questions in order of importance when personally considering accepting a consulting position. Enter "1" in the space provided for the most important question. Complete the rank ordering for remaining questions from the most to least important question.
4. Briefly explain what criteria were important to prioritizing the questions. Why was the No. 1 question selected to be ranked first?

6.3.3 Define Parameters of Effective Consultative Relationships

Title Defining the Role and Scope of Work of a Consultant

Objectives
1. The student will be able to define the role of a consultant.
2. The student will be able to describe a scope of work for a consultant.

Directions
1. Read the following *scenario*.

   A health educator has been asked to serve as an external consultant to a local alcohol abuse prevention coalition. Local data show that underage alcohol use and its consequences are occurring at rates that exceed the state and national rates. The coalition seeks to better understand the attitudes and beliefs of various sectors of the community pertaining to underage alcohol use and its consequences. The health educator recently met with the leadership team of the coalition to assess its consultation needs. The leadership team indicated it would like to achieve the following:

   a. A thorough understanding of the extent of underage alcohol use, how youth gain access to alcohol, the consequences that underage youth experience from alcohol use, attitudes of the community about the severity of underage alcohol use, perceptions of retail and social availability, perceptions of enforcement of underage alcohol use policies and laws

   b. Collection of both survey data and small-group interviews regarding underage alcohol use

   c. A plan to launch an extensive media campaign to reduce underage access to alcohol by targeting youth, parents/adults, faith community, law enforcement, and alcohol vendors.

   Based on the discussion with the leadership team of the coalition about its consulting needs and verification of the qualifications needed for the project, the health educator has agreed to serve as a consultant on this project.

2. Access and read Sections 8 and 9 of Chapter 12 of *The Community Tool Box* (KU Work Group, 2011) (see **Student Resource** for the URL for Chapter 12).

3. Assume the role of the health educator in the *scenario*. After defining the parameters (e.g., role of the consultant, scope of work, and timeline), a logical next step is to gather background information about the organization/group requesting consultation, the community, and the issue of focus for the consultative relationship.

   a. Develop a list of questions to be used to assess the organization/group history, personalities, vision, mission, organizational culture/philosophy, structure, priorities, and funding/resources (KU Work Group for Community Health and Development, 2011).

   b. Develop a list of questions to be used to assess the community's history, personalities, culture, politics, and economics (KU Work Group for Community Health and Development, 2011).

   c. Develop a list of questions to further the understanding of the issue in this scenario and how the issue fits with other purposes of the organization/group requesting consultation (KU Work Group for Community Health and Development, 2011).

   d. Describe some proposed methods (e.g., formal and informal meetings, existing data, interviews, networking) for gathering information to answer each of the questions from **Items a** through **c**. Justify the reasons for the proposed method(s).

Student Resource
The Community Tool Box. Chapter 12, Providing training and technical assistance
http://ctb.ku.edu
Click on the Table of Contents. Scroll to and click on the link for Chapter 12.

Reference
KU Work Group for Community Health and Development. (2011). Providing training and technical assistance. In: *The community tool box* (Chapter 12). Lawrence: University of Kansas. Retrieved from http://ctb.ku.edu/en/tablecontents/chapter_1012.aspx

6.3.4 Establish Consultative Relationships

Title Gather Background Information to Establish Successful Consultative Relationships

Objective The student will be able to gather background information essential for establishing successful consultative relationships.

Directions

1. Access and read Section 9 of Chapter 12 of *The Community Tool Box* (see **Student Resource** for the URL for Chapter 12).
2. Read the *scenario* and complete **Activity 6.3.3**.
3. Assume the role of the health educator in this *scenario*. After defining the parameters (e.g., role of the consultant, scope of work, and timeline), a logical next step is to gather background information about the organization/group requesting consultation, the community, and the issue of focus for the consultative relationship. Prepare a written response to each of the following items that are important steps for gathering background information (KU Work Group for Community Health and Development, 2011):
   a. Develop a list of questions to be used to assess the organization/group history, personalities (e.g., characteristics of turf issues of the main players), vision/mission, organizational culture/philosophy, organizational structure, priorities (e.g., main goals), and funding/resources.
   b. Develop a list of questions to be used to assess the community's history with the organization/group, personalities/influential groups in the community, cultural beliefs about acceptable/unacceptable practices, fit of the organization/group's work within the community, politics, and community economics (e.g., description of income, poverty, and industry).
   c. Develop a list of questions to further the understanding of the issue in this *scenario* and how the issue fits with other purposes of the organization/group requesting consultation.
   d. Describe some proposed methods for gathering information to answer each of the questions from **Items a** through **c** (e.g., informal and formal meetings, existing data, interviews, or networking). Justify the reasons for the proposed method(s).

Student Resource

The Community Tool Box. Chapter 12, Providing training and technical assistance
http://ctb.ku.edu
Click on the Table of Contents. Scroll to and click on the link for Chapter 12.

Reference

KU Work Group for Community Health and Development. (2011). Providing training and technical assistance. In: *The community tool box* (Chapter 12). Lawrence: University of Kansas. Retrieved from http://ctb.ku.edu/en/tablecontents/chapter_1012.aspx

6.3.6 Facilitate Collaborative Efforts to Achieve Program Goals

Title Describing Partner Contributions to Collaborative Efforts

Objective The student will be able to describe how specific partners can contribute to collaborative efforts to achieve program goals.

Directions

1. Access and read Chapter 7 of *The Community Tool Box* (see **Student Resource** for the URL), and/or read information provided by course instructor.
2. Read the *scenario* found for **Activity 6.3.3**.
3. Assume the role of the health educator in this *scenario*. Prepare a written response to the following items, which are samples of activities for building a successful partnership (Olson, 2010):
   a. Develop a one-sentence goal statement for the *scenario*.
   b. Develop a list of potential partners who the coalition can work with to accomplish the goal. This list should be in groups of potential targets of the media campaign (e.g., youth, parents/adults, faith communities, law enforcement, alcohol vendors).
   c. Describe how each of the aforementioned partners identified can contribute to collaborative efforts to achieve program goals. For example, identify their interests in the issue, specific capabilities and resources that the partner possesses, or how the partner fits with the coalition's purpose/goal.
   d. Write an invitation letter to be sent to one of the identified partners inviting that partner to an initial meeting of a potential partnership to address underage alcohol use. The letter should be tailored to the specific partner and should identify how the partner could possibly contribute to collaborative efforts to achieve the program goal.

Student Resource

The Community Tool Box. Chapter 7, Encouraging involvement in community work
http://ctb.ku.edu
Click on the Table of Contents. Scroll to and select Chapter 7.

References

KU Work Group for Community Health and Development. (2011). Encouraging involvement in community work. In: *The community tool box* (Chapter 7). Lawrence: University of Kansas. Retrieved from http://ctb.ku.edu/en/tablecontents/chapter_1006.aspx

Olson, S. J. (2010). Partnerships and collaboration: Critical components to promoting health. In: B. Healey & R. Zimmerman (Eds.). *The new world of health promotion: New program development, implementation, and evaluation* (pp. 290–292). Sudbury, MA: Jones & Bartlett Learning.

6.3.8 Apply Ethical Principles in Consultative Relationships

Title Guidance for Ethical Behavior While Consulting

Objective The student will be able to use the *Code of Ethics for the Health Education Profession* in guiding ethical behavior in consultative relationships.

Directions
1. Read the long version of the *Code of Ethics for the Health Education Profession* as published by the Coalition of National Health Education Organizations (2011).
2. Read the ethical situation and then answer the questions located in **Table 6.3.8-1**.

Student Resources
1. Coalition of National Health Education Organizations (CNHEO). (2011). *Code of ethics for the health education profession.*
   http://www.cnheo.org
2. Read materials provided by the course instructor about ethical decision making.

References
Coalition of National Health Education Organizations (CNHEO). (2011). *Code of ethics for the health education profession.* Retrieved from http://www.cnheo.org

Greenberg, J. S. (2001). *The code of ethics for the health education profession: A case study book.* Sudbury, MA: Jones and Bartlett.

Table 6.3.8-1 Discussing Consultation Reports

The National Institute for Early Childhood Studies (NIECS) sponsors a series of demonstration projects to enhance the chances for low-income children to succeed in school. One of its programs is a Public Broadcasting System television series modeled after *Sesame Street* but targeted specifically to low-income children and their special early learning needs.

   The program has been on the air for 2 years and has been well received by many powerful groups in the community. The program appears to be successful but at a very high cost. Some believe that the money could be better spent on other projects. NIECS has asked for an evaluation of the program's impact. An outside agency has received a contract to do this evaluation. Roger has been given the responsibility of conducting the evaluation in eight key test markets.

   Following the conduct of many focus groups with various target populations and constituencies, individual household telephone interviews in the target markets, and an assessment of the level of penetration into these key markets, several points become clear to Roger:

   1. The program uses high levels of resources.

   2. The program has high visibility among selected power brokers in the community.

   3. The program has very low levels of actual market penetration.

   4. The program receives mixed reactions at the household level.

   Roger concludes that a politically popular program has evolved, for which there is little evidence of satisfaction or benefit at the consumer level. Given the resources expended by the program, Roger recommends that the program be canceled and the resources reallocated.

   Roger turns in his report to NIECS, and the evaluation is promptly "buried." Roger feels that his evaluation was designed to make recommendations, but it is up to NIECS to make decisions. Therefore, it is his right to bury the report and continue the program in spite of the evidence.

Answer these questions about this ethical situation:

   1. What ethical issue is raised in this scenario?

   2. What is the responsibility of an individual to make known the results of evaluation studies?

(continues)

Table 6.3.8-1 Discussing Consultation Reports *(continued)*

3. What is the responsibility of a sponsor to make known the results of an evaluation of a publicly funded program?

4. It is possible that NIECS had additional data beyond Roger's report and made a legitimate decision based on all the data. On the other hand, what role does the public's right to know play in this case?

5. How does the *Code of Ethics for the Health Education Profession* address this situation? Name the relevant article(s) and section(s) that apply to this scenario.

6. What could one change or do differently to make an ethical decision?

Reprinted with permission from Greenberg, J. S. (2001). *The code of ethics for the health education profession: A case study book* (pp. 81–82). Sudbury, MA: Jones and Bartlett.

Communicate and Advocate for Health and Health Education

INTRODUCTION

This chapter teaches communication and advocacy through 31 activities that address the 36 entry-level sub-competencies in Area of Responsibility VII.

Students will be challenged to communicate current health policies to the public and advocate for the improvement of health laws and policies from a socio-ecologic perspective. Activities will provide opportunities to identify the best communication channel, tailor messages to a priority population, and develop the message. Activities will also enhance students' understanding of advocacy and the role of the health educator in advocating for better health. These activities will require students to expand their knowledge on topics such as the development of talking points for legislators regarding health legislation, hands-free cell phone use, Healthy People 2020, social media, prevention of concussions in school athletics, sun safety, and healthy food in school vending machines.

Activities will assist students in understanding the components or skills needed for developing a communication campaign and identifying the benefits of social media campaigns. Students will be challenged to develop an advocacy plan for a health issue. Also, they will develop a personal plan for professional growth, explaining the health educator's role in society, and engaging in professional growth activities. Students will engage in mentoring and will contribute to the health education profession through a number of activities.

Students will practice using a variety of interactive media tools, such as video production and PowerPoint or similar presentations, to provide health information tailored to specific populations. They will engage in media advocacy to influence policy makers. Other activities include using data from the *County Health Rankings* or *Community Health Status Indicators* to demonstrate the public health burden of issues and practicing communication skills in a service activity.

For this text, please go to the student companion website at **go.jblearning.com/PracticalApp** to complete activities using e-templates, and then pass your completed activities to your instructor for review of grading.

COMPETENCY 7.1 ASSESS AND PRIORITIZE HEALTH INFORMATION AND ADVOCACY NEEDS

7.1.1 Identify Current and Emerging Issues that May Influence Health and Health Education

7.1.2 Access Accurate Resources Related to Identified Issues

Title Providing Evidence-Based Key Information Supporting a Safety Issue

Objectives
1. The student will be able to identify credible sources to locate evidence-based information.
2. The student will be able to develop talking points to support a current safety and health issue.

Directions
1. Read the *scenario* that follows.
   Assume the role of a student completing an internship at the state health department. A legislator called and requested talking points for an upcoming meeting discussing a new bill under consideration. The bill states only hands-free cell phone usage will be allowed for any licensed individual driving a vehicle within the state borders. The legislator is favorable toward the restrictive safety measure and wants to present evidence-based information to support her position. The internship supervisor has requested research about cell phone usage while driving.
2. Discuss information about finding valid and reliable resources provided by the instructor.
3. Review the four sites listed in **Student Resources** that are helpful to create talking points about the issue of cell phone usage while driving.
4. Identify eight of the most current talking points that are supported by current evidence-based information.

Table 7.1.1-1 Evidenced-Based Talking Points

Talking points with details and complete references
1.
2.
3.
4.
5.
6.
7.
8.
Describe three communication methods to share findings with the legislator.

5. Use **Table 7.1.1-1** to organize and enter the information. Write several sentences that elaborate upon each talking point to strengthen the legislator's ability to influence others. Include a complete reference so the legislator knows the source if asked.

6. List and justify three effective ways to communicate to the legislator the eight talking points, including detailed information, in **Table 7.1.1-1**.

Student Resources

1. AAA Foundation for Safety
   http://www.aaafoundation.org
   In the search box, type "distracted driving."

2. Distraction.Gov, U.S Department of Transportation
   http://www.distraction.gov

3. Insurance Institute for Highway Safety
   http://www.iihs.org
   In the search box, type "distracted driving."

4. National Safety Council
   http://www.nsc.org
   Click on the tab "safety on the road."
   On the left column, select "distracted driving."

7.1.3 Analyze the Impact of Existing and Proposed Policies on Health

Title The Impact of Healthy People 2020 on Health-Related Policies

Objective The student will be able to describe how *Healthy People 2020* will influence decisions concerning health promotion and disease prevention in the next decade.

Directions
Background of Healthy People

The *Healthy People* document is an example of national health guidelines that impacts and gives direction to our nation's health. Every 10 years, this document is revised to better address emerging health issues.

1. Utilize the Healthy People 2020 website provided in **Student Resource**.
2. Complete this activity by answering the series of questions concerning Healthy People 2020, the new goals and objectives to guide national health promotion and disease prevention to improve the health of all people for the future. Length of responses will vary from a single word to several sentences.

Questions
    a. What was the first document instrumental in the process of creating Healthy People?

    b. Following the first document, how many times has it been revised?

    c. After reviewing *Healthy People 2020*, what are three new topics that would be most interesting to an entry-level health educator?

    d. Select one of the new topics listed in **Question c** that is very important to a health educator's work. What is the goal of that topic?

    e. Identity one of the objectives for the selected topic area. What is the baseline? What is the target?

    f. Predict how health promotion and disease prevention effort will be impacted by this new topic in Healthy People 2020.

    g. In what ways can today's health educators take action to prepare for future implementation of Healthy People 2020?

Student Resource
U.S. Department of Human Services (2011). *Healthy People 2020.*
http://healthypeople.gov

7.1.4 Analyze Factors that Influence Decision-Makers

Title Social Media: A Tool for Public Health?

Objective The student will be able to defend a position on mandatory helmet laws through use of social media.

Directions

1. Read the following *scenario*.
   A letter to the editor of a local newspaper addressed Facebook use to spread information about a proposed bill in the state legislature. The proposed bill mandates helmet use when riding a motorcycle. The writer first indicates that mandatory helmet use is wrong because it interferes with personal freedom. The writer then indicates that using Facebook to share information is a joke as it mostly spreads gossip and rumors.
2. Write a letter to the editor in response to the letter in the scenario by first following the guidelines on format, length, and other details of writing and submitting a letter to the editor. The instructor will provide information on the guidelines.
3. Develop content of the letter using three paragraphs.
   a. *Paragraph 1.* State support for mandatory helmets for motorcycle riders. Indicate the interest in this topic as a private citizen or a health educator.
   b. *Paragraph 2.* Provide evidence-based programs, statistics, or other material to support the position held on mandatory use of a Department of Transportation (DOT)-approved helmet while a motorcyclist is riding.
   c. *Paragraph 3.* Emphasize the value of social media, such as Facebook, as a method of sharing information and to rally support to the proposed law.
4. In a separate document, list in APA style a minimum of five references, including at least one government source and two Facebook sources.

Student Resources

1. Advocates for Highway & Auto Safety
   http://wwwsaferoads.org
   In the search box, type "motorcycle helmets."
2. Insurance Institute for Highway Safety
   http://www.iihs.org
   In the search box, type "motorcycle helmets."
3. Motorcycle Riders Foundation
   http://www.mrf.org
   In the search box, type "motorcycle helmets."
4. National Highway Traffic Safety Administration
   http://nhtsa.gov
   In the search box, type "motorcycle helmets."

COMPETENCY 7.2 IDENTIFY AND DEVELOP A VARIETY OF COMMUNICATION STRATEGIES, METHODS, AND TECHNIQUES

7.2.1 Create Messages Using Communication Theories and Models

Title Health Belief Model and Concussion Prevention Messages

Objective The student will be able to use the Health Belief Model to create specific health message.

Directions

1. Read the following *scenario.*

   A group of health educators are working on a campaign to create awareness about sports-related concussions in their community. They want to focus on how to recognize signs and symptoms; short-, intermediate-, and long-term management of the concussion; and ultimately, prevention of concussions. They have decided to target coaches, athletes, parents, and school nurses. Specifically, they want to influence coaches to move toward adopting new techniques and procedures used in practice and games that can help prevent concussions; help athletes understand the importance of reporting a concussion; convince athletes that their peers are reporting on a regular basis; increase parents' awareness of the significance of a concussion and consequences of allowing their child to return to play; and encourage school nurses to learn the symptoms and understand the benefits of taking action when a concussion occurs.

2. Review the information presented about the Health Belief Model from the National Cancer Institute (see **Student Resources**).

3. Select one of the target audiences listed in the *scenario.* Identify a component (perceived susceptibility, perceived seriousness, perceived benefits, perceived barriers, cues to action, or self-efficacy) of the Health Belief Model that would be a good fit for the target audience selected and the behavior presented in the *scenario.* See the following example for school nurses below:

Sample

   Target audience: School nurses
   Health belief model component: Perceived benefits of action—immediate assessment and recognition of a concussion are important in preventing further injury and for post-concussion management
   Target audience:

   Health belief model component:

4. Outline a message that incorporates the focus suggested in the *scenario.* For now, write a summary or outline of the message. Use the health belief model component to guide the content of your message. See the following example for the school nurse below:

Sample

   Target audience: School nurses
   Message: Many concussions occur during school activities where there is the possibility of collisions, such as during a physical education class, on the playground, at recess, or during

a school-based sports activity. The message should incorporate statistics about how many concussions occur during school and should provide the scientific data regarding the importance of taking immediate action to assess and manage a concussion event.

Target audience:

Message:

Student Resources

1. National Cancer Institute
   http://www.cancer.gov
   Type "theory" in the search box, and click on "Theory at a glance. A guide for health promotion practice."
2. Centers for Disease Control and Prevention
   http://www.cdc.gov
   In the search box, type "Traumatic brain injury."
3. Centers for Disease Control and Prevention
   http://www.cdc.gov
   Type "health communication" into the search box, and find "Gateway to Health Communication and Social Marketing Practice."

7.2.2 Tailor Messages to Priority Populations

Title Audience Insight

Objective The student will be able to use target audience analysis for creating health messages.

Directions

1. For this activity, the focus of a health campaign is sun safety. Use of the Audience Insight tool identified at the CDC's Gateway to Health Communication & Social Marketing Practice will be necessary for successful completion of this activity. See **Student Resources** and access the site.

2. Summarize some of the key points from the Audience Insight tool for each of the target groups listed below the *sample* that would be helpful in designing health message about sun safety. This might include habits, values, and demographics. Be sure to scroll all the way through the document to view all of the information provided for the specific target group. Avoid mention of the channels for delivery such as use of technology and the media, e.g., TV and Internet. Follow the *sample* provided.

Sample

The responsible generation: Engage in gardening as a leisure activity where they are exposed to the sun; core values include family and commitment; women outnumber men; respect authority; preventing disease is a priority.

Moms:

Teens:

Boomers:

3. Select one of the audiences (moms, teens, or boomers).
4. Create a simple message that emphasizes sun safety. The message should include at least five points that reflect or connect to the key points summarized in **Step 2**. Follow the *sample* provided in **Table 7.2.2-1**.
5. Use the resources provided in **Student Resources** for content.

Student Resources

1. Centers for Disease Control and Prevention Audience Insight
   http://www.cdc.gov
   Type "health communication" into the search box to locate "Gateway to Health Communication and Social Marketing Practice."
   Click on "audience" to go to the Audience Insight tool.
2. Centers for Disease Control and Prevention
   http://www.cdc.gov
   Type "skin cancer" in the search box, and click on the Search button.

Table 7.2.2-1 Sun Safety Message

Sample Audience: The Responsible Generation	Audience:
Message Outline: 1. Protect you and your family from the sun 2. Avoid the sun—get in the shade when possible 3. Wear a hat with a broad rim 4. Use sunscreen even on cloudy days 5. Work in the garden before 10 a.m. or after 3 p.m.	Message Outline:

3. Environmental Protection Agency
   http://www.epa.gov
   Type "sunwise" in the search box, and click on the Search button.

7.2.3 Incorporate Images to Enhance Messages

Title A Picture Is Worth A Thousand Words

Objective The student will be able to identify a variety of graphics to enhance health messages.

Directions
1. Use the target audience selected in **Activity 7.2.2** and the topic of sun safety for this assignment.
2. Do an Internet search for photos, images, or clip art that would be appropriate for the target audience and topic.
3. Create an electronic file with the materials.
4. Make a list of the sources where the materials were located. Grouping like materials will facilitate organizing and accessing graphics more efficiently.
5. Select two of the graphics that best represent "A picture is worth a thousand words" and explain why each was selected over all others.

Student Resources
1. Sunsafety
   http://www.sunsafety.qld.gov.au
   Click on any of the tabs and find the "Image Library."
2. CDC Public Health Image Library
   http://phil.cdc.gov/phil/home.asp
3. Sun Safety Alliance
   http://www.sunsafetyalliance.org
4. Sun protection
   http://www.edupics.com
   Use the keywords "sun protection."

7.2.4 Select Effective Methods or Channels for Communicating to Priority Populations

Title How to Say It: Selecting the Right Channel

Objective The student will be able to identify appropriate channels for communicating health messages for a specific target audience.

Directions
This activity will incorporate assignments completed in **Activity 7.2.2** and **Activity 7.2.3**.
1. Use the target audience selected for **Activity 7.2.2** (moms, teens, or boomers).
2. Review the Audience Insight tool for the target audience selected and the Channels link at the CDC's Gateway to Health Communication & Social Marketing Practice page listed in **Student Resources**.
3. Select two channels that would be a good approach for delivering health messages to the target group. Write a brief narrative summary of the channels recommended and why they would be a good choice. See the *sample* provided.

Sample
Target audience: Responsible Generation
Summary of channels: The responsible generation has close connections to the faith-based community. Health messages could be delivered through displays at the faith-based community meeting places or incorporated into the newsletters or other methods of communication used by these groups. The responsible generation is less likely to use social media but will use the Internet to locate health information. Setting up an easily navigable website with information could be a useful channel for this group.

4. Incorporate the sun safety message created in **Activity 7.2.2**, **Table 7.2.2-1** into a "channel" as described in the *sample*. If applicable, use the images collected in **Activity 7.2.3**. If a web-based channel is selected (such as a web page, blog, podcast, or YouTube clip), create the product and provide a link. If other channels are used (print media such as posters, flyers, or press releases), attach a copy.

Student Resources
1. Centers for Disease Control and Prevention, Audience Insight
   http://www.cdc.gov
   Type "health communication" into the search box, click on the Search button, and click on "Gateway to Health Communication & Social Marketing Practice." Click on "Audience" and go to the Audience Insight tool.
2. Centers for Disease Control and Prevention, Channels
   http://www.cdc.gov
   Type "health communication" into the search box, click on the Search button, and select "Gateway to Health Communication & Social Marketing Practice." Click on the Channels link.

7.2.5 Pilot Test Messages and Delivery Methods on Priority Populations

7.2.6 Revise Messages Based on Pilot Feedback

Title Does the Health Message Delivery Method Work?

Objectives
1. The student will be able to pilot test a health communication message.
2. The student will be able to revise a health communication message based on target audience feedback.

Directions
1. Use the final product from **Activity 7.2.4**.
2. Identify at least three individuals from the target audience for which the message in **Activity 7.2.4** was designed.
3. Share the final product with individuals selected.
4. Ask for their feedback for the following questions:
   a. *Message content.* Was the message easy to understand? Did the message contain too much information? Was it appropriate for adults? If not, why?
   b. *Design.* Was the design attention getting? Was it easy to navigate (if applicable)?
   c. *Outcome.* Was the message impactful? Was it motivating? Will it be appropriate to share it with other adults?
5. Summarize the comments.
6. Revise the product based upon the input received from participants.

COMPETENCY 7.3 DELIVER MESSAGES USING A VARIETY OF STRATEGIES, METHODS, AND TECHNIQUES

7.3.1 Use Techniques that Empower Individuals and Communities to Improve Their Health

7.3.2 Employ Technology to Communicate to Priority Populations

7.3.3 Evaluate the Delivery of Communication Strategies, Methods, and Techniques

Title Kicking Butts: Improving the Environment One Cigarette Butt at a Time

Objectives

1. The student will be able to use photography to communicate environmental health issues.
2. The student will be able to use electronic media to create awareness of a health issue.
3. The student will be able to design a feedback technique for evaluating an electronic communication message.

Directions

1. Review the information in **Student Resources** about cigarette litter issues.
2. Identify a setting that is accessible. Examples might be a university campus, a neighborhood, a place of work, or a shopping center. The target audience is adults.
3. Take four to six pictures of areas in the selected environment that are obvious problem areas for cigarette butt litter. Do not take photos of people. Concentrate on objects.
4. Using the photos and information gathered from the cigarette litter issues in **Student Resources**, create a podcast, website, Facebook page, YouTube broadcast, widget, or other form of electronic (digital) media to illustrate the problem of cigarette butt litter.
5. To evaluate the product, write three questions that could be used to obtain feedback from the target audience.
6. Arrange for time to show the created product to at least five adults. Try to have a diverse representation of gender, race, and age.
7. Ask participants to answer the three evaluation questions.
8. Summarize the participants' responses in a short paragraph. Include strengths and weaknesses of the product with suggestions for improvements.

Student Resources

1. Guide to Cigarette Litter Prevention
   http://www.preventcigarettelitter.org
2. Cigarettelitter.org
   http://www.cigarettelitter.org

COMPETENCY 7.4 ENGAGE IN HEALTH EDUCATION ADVOCACY

7.4.1 Engage Stakeholders in Advocacy

Title Building a Stakeholder Base for Health Education Advocacy

Objectives
1. The student will be able to explain a health education advocacy issue.
2. The student will be able to identify the allies and opponents of a health education advocacy issue.
3. The student will be able to build a stakeholder base for a health education advocacy issue.

Directions
1. Identify a health education advocacy issue by searching for the term *advocacy* or *policy* from within the web page of one of the following professional or nongovernmental organizations:
   a. American Alliance for Health, Physical Education, Recreation, and Dance
   b. American Cancer Society
   c. American Heart Association
   d. American Public Health Association
   e. Community Anti-Drug Coalitions of America
   f. The Society for Public Health Education

   Examples of a health education advocacy issue are supporting safe routes to school, supporting healthier school lunches, and making a case against the legalization of marijuana.
2. Access and read Sections 3, 4, and 5 of Chapter 30 and Section 4 of Chapter 31 of *The Community Tool Box* (2011a, 2011b; see **Students Resources** for the URLs) to learn about methods of understanding the issue and identifying the allies and opponents of health education advocacy issues.
3. Conduct background research on the identified health education advocacy issue and record the findings in **Table 7.4.1-1**.
4. Use **Table 7.4.1-2** to prepare a list of stakeholders who should be engaged in advocacy efforts for the health education advocacy issue described in **Table 7.4.1-1**.

Table 7.4.1-1 Background Research of Health Education Advocacy Issue

What is the health education advocacy issue? What are the main points of the issue?
What source(s) of information were used to conduct background research?
Who is affected by the advocacy issue?
What are the consequences of the advocacy issue?
Who are the allies on the issue?

Table 7.4.1-1 Background Research of Health Education Advocacy Issue *(continued)*

What is the common ground that is shared by the allies?
Who are the opponents of the issue?

Adapted from KU Work Group for Community Health and Development. (2011). Principles of advocacy. In: *The community tool box* (Chapter 30). Lawrence: University of Kansas. Retrieved from http://ctb.ku.edu/en/tablecontents/chapter_1030.aspx

Table 7.4.1-2 List of Stakeholders to Engage in Advocacy

The following stakeholders should be engaged in the advocacy efforts for the issue identified in **Table 7.4.1-1.**

1.

2.

3.

4.

5.

6.

Student Resources

1. *The Community Tool Box.* Chapter 30, Principles of advocacy
   http://ctb.ku.edu
   Click on the Table of Contents and then scroll to and click on the link for Chapter 30.
2. *The Community Tool Box.* Chapter 31, Conducting advocacy research
   http://ctb.ku.edu
   Click on the Table of Contents and then scroll to and click on the link for Chapter 31.

References

KU Work Group for Community Health and Development. (2011a). Conducting advocacy research. In: *The community tool box* (Chapter 31). Lawrence: University of Kansas. Retrieved from http://ctb.ku.edu/en/tablecontents/chapter_1031.aspx

KU Work Group for Community Health and Development. (2011b). Principles of advocacy. In: *The community tool box* (Chapter 30). Lawrence: University of Kansas. Retrieved from http://ctb.ku.edu/en/tablecontents/chapter_1030.aspx

7.4.2 Develop an Advocacy Plan in Compliance with Local, State, and/or Federal Policies and Procedures

Title Planning for Advocacy: Essential Components and Restrictions

Objectives
1. The student will be able to explain the essential components of an advocacy plan.
2. The student will be aware of the restrictions for advocacy activities for those employed or funded by the federal government.

Directions
1. Complete **Activity 7.4.1**.
2. Access and read Section 7 of Chapter 30 from *The Community Tool Box* to learn about components of an advocacy plan. See **Student Resources** for the URL.
3. Describe in one short paragraph each of the six components of an advocacy plan listed in **Table 7.4.2-1**.
4. Use the health advocacy issue identified in **Activity 7.4.1** and conduct further background research about the goals, targets and agents of change, and strategies. Explain the advocacy plan for the identified issue in **Table 7.4.2-2**.
5. Access the National Institutes of Health Ethics Program website using the URL provided in **Student Resources**.
6. Use a search engine to conduct a search for the Anti-Lobbying Act, 18 U.S.C. § 1913.
7. Use **Table 7.4.2-3** to describe the Anti-Lobbying Act and to discuss the implications on the advocacy plan outline in **Table 7.4.2-2**.

Student Resources
1. *The Community Tool Box.* Chapter 30, Principles of advocacy
   http://ctb.ku.edu
   Click on the Table of Contents and then scroll to and click on the link for Chapter 30.
2. National Institutes of Health Ethics Program
   http://ethics.od.nih.gov

Table 7.4.2-1 Description of Components of Advocacy Plan

Component of Advocacy Plan	Description of Component
Goals (or objectives)	
Resources and assets	
Community support	

Table 7.4.2-1 Description of Components of Advocacy Plan *(continued)*

Targets and agents of change	
Planning the strategies	
Tactics	

Adapted from KU Work Group for Community Health and Development. (2011). Principles of advocacy. In: *The community tool box* (Chapter 30). Lawrence: University of Kansas. Retrieved from http://ctb.ku.edu/en/tablecontents/chapter_1030.aspx

Table 7.4.2-2 Advocacy Plan: Goals, Targets and Agents of Change, and Strategies

What is the health education advocacy issue?
What source(s) of information were used to conduct background research?
What is the ultimate goal of the advocacy issue?
What is the immediate objective of the advocacy issue?
Who are the targets of change? What individuals or entities need to alter behavior to achieve the goal?

(continues)

Table 7.4.2-2 Advocacy Plan: Goals, Targets and Agents of Change, and Strategies *(continued)*

Who are the agents of change? Who will cause the targets to change/alter behavior?
What strategies are used to achieve the goal(s) (for example, a media campaign, education, or networking)?

Adapted from KU Work Group for Community Health and Development. (2011). Principles of advocacy. In: *The community tool box* (Chapter 30). Lawrence: University of Kansas. Retrieved from http://ctb.ku.edu/en/tablecontents/chapter_1030.aspx

Table 7.4.2-3 The Anti-Lobbying Act and Implications for an Advocacy Plan

What is the Anti-Lobbying Act? What types of activities does the Anti-Lobbying Act restrict?
Assume that some of the agents of change from the selected advocacy issue are federal employees. Does this impact their ability to conduct advocacy activities while on the job? If so, how?
Assume that some of the agents of change from the selected advocacy issue work for an agency that has a contract or receives a grant from the federal government. Does this impact their ability to conduct advocacy activities while on the job? If so, how?

United States Department of Health and Human Services, National Institute of Health Ethics Program. (2011). *Lobbying and publicity or propaganda guidelines*. Retrieved from http://ethics.od.nih.gov/topics/Lobby-Publicity-Guide.htm

References

KU Work Group for Community Health and Development. (2011). Principles of advocacy. In: *The community tool box* (Chapter 30). Lawrence: University of Kansas. Retrieved from http://ctb.ku.edu/en/tablecontents/chapter_1030.aspx

United States Department of Health and Human Services, National Institute of Health Ethics Program. (2011). *Lobbying and publicity or propaganda guidelines*. Retrieved from http://ethics.od.nih.gov/topics/Lobby-Publicity-Guide.htm

7.4.3 Comply with Organizational Policies Related to Participating in Advocacy

Title Participating in Advocacy: Maintaining Compliance with Organizational Policies

Objectives

1. The student will be able to describe organizational policies related to participating in advocacy.
2. The student will be able to explain how to maintain a balance between obligation to the profession and compliance with organizational polices related to participating in advocacy.

Directions

1. Consult with the course instructor to develop a list of local nonprofit, nongovernmental, and/or local and state public health organizations for the purpose of contacting them about organizational policies related to participating in advocacy.
2. Contact the program administrator of at least three of the identified agencies either via telephone or email. Explain the purpose of the communication is to learn more about organizational policies related to participating in advocacy.
3. Ask the following questions of the program administrator from each of the three identified agencies:
   a. Does your organization have a formal policy on employee participation in advocacy activities while on organizational time?
   b. If yes, what are the guidelines or restrictions for the organization and employee engagement in advocacy activities?
   c. Is your agency a governmental, nongovernmental, nonprofit, for-profit, or other type of agency?
   d. How is your agency funded? Private? Service fees? Governmental funds? Other?
4. Send a thank-you note to the program administrator following the telephone or email interview.
5. Compare and contrast the answers to the questions from each of the three agencies. Note if there are differences in organizational policies according to the type of agency or type of funding received.
6. Read the following *scenario*.
   Assume the role of a health educator employed by an organization with a policy prohibiting an employee from engaging in advocacy while on organizational time. The *Code of Ethics for the Health Education Profession* encourages the health educator to support actions that have greater benefit than harm and that promote, maintain, and improve individual, family, and community health (CNHEO, 2011). As an individual citizen and a member of a professional association, the health educator can engage in advocacy.
7. Describe how the health educator can balance compliance with organizational policies and engagement in advocacy as a citizen and on behalf of a professional organization.

Reference

Coalition of National Health Education Organizations (CNHEO). (2011). *Code of ethics for the health education profession*. Retrieved from http://www.cnheo.org/PDF%20files/CODE%20OF%20ETHICS%202011%20Full.pdf

7.4.4 Communicate the Impact of Health and Health Education on Organizational and Socio-Ecological Factors

Title Communicating the Role of Health Educators from a Socio-Ecological Perspective

Objective The student will be able to communicate the role of health educators in planning and implementing strategies from a socio-ecological perspective.

Directions

1. Read material provided by the course instructor about the ecological model.
2. Respond to the following *scenario*.
   A health educator who has been working in the profession for about 2 years has been asked by the agency administration to develop a one-page handout about the role of health educators in generating policy changes that lead to creating optimal health of populations by addressing multiple determinants of health. This presentation will be used at job recruitment events and will be placed on the agency website.
3. Assume the role of the health educator. Develop a handout that describes policy initiatives/ environmental strategies used to impact health at the individual, organizational, institutional, economical, societal, and political levels. The handout should clearly outline the role of the health educator in this process.

Student Resource

Material is provided by the course instructor about the ecological model.

7.4.5 Use Data to Support Advocacy Messages

Title Show Public Health Burden of an Advocacy Issue

Objective The student will be able to assemble data to show the public health burden of an advocacy issue.

Directions

1. Complete **Activities 7.4.1** and **7.4.2**.
2. Use the advocacy issue identified in **Activity 7.4.1**. Assume that the impact of the targeted advocacy issue is at the county level. Select a state and a county as the target population for the advocacy issue.
3. Access county level data through either *County Health Rankings* or *Community Health Status Indicators* (see **Student Resources** for URLs) to show the public health burden of the advocacy issue. The data should be specific to the advocacy issue and may include morbidity statistics (e.g., prevalence or incidence of injury, illness, or disease, years of life lost, or absenteeism), mortality statistics of the health problem, and/or risk factors of the targeted issue. Compare the data gathered from the county level to state and/or national level as a benchmark.
4. Write a two- to three-paragraph description of the public health burden of the advocacy issue. Identify the advocacy issue, cite specific statistics demonstrating the public health burden, and explain why this issue should be a priority over other issues (e.g., how the county level data compares to the state level data).

Student Resources

1. University of Wisconsin Population Health Institute, Robert Wood Johnson Foundation. (2011). *County health rankings*.
http://www.countyhealthrankings.org
2. United States Department of Health & Human Services. (2009). *Community health status indicators report*.
http://communityhealth.hhs.gov

7.4.6 Implement Advocacy Plans

Title Develop Tactics to Achieve Advocacy Campaign Goals

Objective The student will be able to develop tactics to influence advocacy targets to help achieve the advocacy goal.

Directions

1. Complete **Activities 7.4.1** and **7.4.2**.
2. Access and read all sections of Chapter 33 of *The Community Tool Box* (see **Student Resource** for the URL) to learn about various tactics of an advocacy campaign.
3. Select at least three tactics that can be implemented as part of the advocacy plan that was developed in **Activity 7.4.2**.
4. Describe each selected tactic in one paragraph and explain how each tactic will help achieve the advocacy goal as outlined in the advocacy plan developed in **Activity 7.4.2**. Record the responses in **Table 7.4.6-1**.

Table 7.4.6-1 Description of Advocacy Tactics and Relation to Goal(s)

Description of Tactic	Description of How Tactic Will Help Achieve Advocacy Goal(s)
Tactic No. 1:	
Tactic No. 2:	
Tactic No. 3:	

Student Resource

The Community Tool Box. Chapter 33, Conducting a direct action campaign
http://ctb.ku.edu
Click on Table of Contents and then scroll to and click on the link for Chapter 33.

Reference

KU Work Group for Community Health and Development. (2011). Conducting a direct action campaign. In: *The community tool box* (Chapter 33). Lawrence: University of Kansas. Retrieved from http://ctb.ku.edu/en/tablecontents/chapter_1033.aspx

7.4.7 Incorporate Media and Technology in Advocacy

Title Use of Technology in Advocacy

Objective The student will be able to utilize technology when working on advocacy issues.

Directions
1. Complete **Activity 7.4.6**.
2. Access the e-advocacy tools that are listed in **Student Resource**.
3. Demonstrate the use of the e-advocacy tools by locating the information requested in **Table 7.4.7-1**.
4. Explain, in **Table 7.4.7-2**, how the e-advocacy tools can be used in implementing the tactics described in **Activities 7.4.6**.

Student Resource
American Public Health Association
http://action.apha.org
Click on "Advocacy and tools."

Table 7.4.7-1 Demonstrating Informational Finds Using E-Advocacy Tools

Information Items to Search Using E-Advocacy Tools	Information Found Using E-Advocacy Tools
Names of U.S. senators and district contact information	
Name of U.S. representative and district contact information	
Recent political vote of either the senator or the representative (list the bill and the vote)	
Name and contact information of one national media organization	
Name and contact information of one local newspaper	
One election race currently taking place	

Table 7.4.7-2 How E-Advocacy Tools Can Be Used

Tactic Description (from Activity 7.4.6)	Description of How E-Advocacy Tools Can Be Used for the Tactic
1.	
2.	
3.	

7.4.8 Participate in Advocacy Initiatives

Title Contact a Policy Maker

Objective The student will be able to conduct direct lobbying by contacting a policy maker.

Directions
1. Complete **Activities 7.4.1** through **7.4.7**.
2. Access and read Section 1 of Chapter 33 from *The Community Tool Box* to learn about writing letters to elected officials. See **Student Resource** for the URL.
3. Identify a policy maker to whom a letter can be written to directly lobby for/against the advocacy issue identified in **Activity 7.4.1**.
4. Use the e-advocacy tools described in **Activity 7.4.7** to locate the contact information for a legislator (United States or state), if appropriate. If the policy maker is local, use a local directory or contact the local government office to obtain the contact information.
5. Write a letter to the policy maker addressing the selected advocacy issue. To increase the likelihood that the letter will actually be read and taken seriously, use the following guidelines for writing letters to policy makers as described in *The Community Tool Box* (2011):
   a. Decide on the recipient and have proper recipient address and correct spelling of names.
   b. Use an official opening with date, respectful title, and full address.
   c. Explain the purpose of the communication.
   d. Discuss the general (summary) impact of the issue.
   e. State and explain your personal position on the issue.
   f. Describe what any changes in the issue will mean personally.
   g. Identify those affected and show the public health burden by using data (see **Activity 7.4.5**).
   h. Acknowledge the policy maker's previous support of policy issues, if applicable.
   i. Describe the desired action of the policy maker or offer an alternative if the purpose is to oppose a previous action.
   j. Close the letter and sign the letter, including the appropriate contact information.
   k. Review, check spelling and grammar, and revise.
6. Obtain instructor approval of the letter.
7. Submit the letter via email or U.S. mail to the policy maker, if the timing is appropriate.

Student Resource
The Community Tool Box. Chapter 33, Conducting a direct action campaign
http://ctb.ku.edu
Click on Table of Contents and then scroll to and click on the link for Chapter 33.

Reference
KU Work Group for Community Health and Development. (2011). Conducting a direct action campaign. In: *The community tool box* (Chapter 33). Lawrence: University of Kansas. Retrieved from http://ctb.ku.edu/en/tablecontents/chapter_1033.aspx

COMPETENCY 7.5 INFLUENCE POLICY TO PROMOTE HEALTH

7.5.2 Identify the Significance and Implications of Health Policy for Individuals, Groups, and Communities

Title School Vending Machine Policies: Implications for Different Constituents

Objective The student will be able to identify how a policy change may affect diverse groups.

Directions

1. Read the following *scenario*.

   After years of offering snacks and soft drinks in vending machines, administrators of a school district are considering the removal of machines. This policy change has created much controversy among students, teachers, parents, cafeteria staff, and administrators. Groups like the parent–teacher organization (PTO) also have voiced opinions. The superintendent of schools has organized a series of meetings to allow individuals and groups to share their concerns before a decision is made. The superintendent has contacted the public health department requesting a health educator who could attend the meetings to present evidence-based research findings, both pros and cons on removing the vending machines, and how policy affects individuals, groups, and the school district overall. Assume the role of the public health department health educator.

2. Use **Table 7.5.2-1** to record current evidence-based research (see **Student Resources** for a starting point for content) according to its relevance and effects upon the categories of individuals, groups, or communities (e.g., school district, town/city).

3. Cite the references parenthetically in text and include a complete list (APA style) of references at end of the table.

4. For the meetings, develop a PowerPoint presentation (or a similar presentation) based on the information in **Table 7.5.2-1**. Share the most important arguments by categories for keeping or removing the schools' soft drink vending machines.

Table 7.5.2-1 Policy Change Decision for Removal of School Vending Machines

Categories of Affected People	Evidence-Based Research with Reference Citations	
Individuals (student)	Pros	
	Cons	
Groups (teachers)	Pros	
	Cons	

(continues)

Table 7.5.2-1 Policy Change Decision for Removal of School Vending Machines *(continued)*

Cafeteria staff	Pros	
	Cons	
PTO	Pros	
	Cons	
Communities (school district, town, or city)	Pros	
	Cons	
References for research		

Student Resources

1. Action for Healthy Kids
   http://www.actionforhealthykids.org
   In the search box, type "vending machines."
2. School-based Obesity Strategies for State Policymakers
   http://www.cdc.gov
   In the search box, type "school vending machines."

7.5.3 Advocate for Health-Related Policies, Regulations, Laws, or Rules

7.5.5 Employ Policy and Media Advocacy Techniques to Influence Decision-Makers

Title Using Email as an Efficient and Effective Advocacy Technique

Objectives

1. The student will be able to develop a business email to communicate a position on a health-related issue.
2. The student will be able to distinguish the best mode of communication among email, telephone, and letter.

Directions

1. Select from the list an area of interest. Another topic may be acceptable with instructor approval.
   a. Eliminating all cell phone texting while driving any motor vehicle
   b. Encouraging each state to adopt year-round education in all public school districts
   c. Establishing policies on athletic practices during extreme heat
   d. Requiring nutritional information be available at all fast food restaurants
2. Discuss why emailing legislators is a preferred method for advocating a specific position on a very controversial issue or a proposed bill still in committee or pending state or federal legislation.
3. Review the instructor's directions and guidelines on how to write a business email.
4. Use **Table 7.5.3-1** to organize the evidence needed for advocacy before beginning to write an email to a state legislator or U.S. senator or House representative.
5. Develop an email to a legislator following the business email format, and these guidelines:
   a. State clearly the position being advocated.
   b. Provide sufficient, impactful evidence.
   c. Identify what is desired of the legislator, e.g., vote for a specific bill.
   d. End by thanking the legislator and indicating a response would be appreciated.
   e. Include your name and a street address with town/city so the legislator knows the email is from a constituent.
6. Suppose several weeks later that a response is received from the legislator. Write a second email to acknowledge and thank the legislator for the response.

Table 7.5.3-1 Evidence Supporting an Advocacy Position

Topic of interest:	
Advocacy position of support or opposition:	
Evidence for Selected Advocacy Position	**In-Text Reference**
1.	
2.	
3.	

(continues)

Table 7.5.3-1 Evidence Supporting an Advocacy Position *(continued)*

4.	
5.	
6.	
References	

Student Resources

1. The White House
   http://www.whitehouse.gov
   Click on the Contact Us link in the upper right corner.
2. Distracted Driving
   http://www.distraction.gov
3. National Association for Year-round Education
   http://www.nayre.org
4. Centers for Disease Control and Prevention
   http://www.cdc.gov
   In the search box, type "heat illness among high school athletes."
5. The Federal Register
   http://www.federalregister.gov
   In the search box, type "restaurant food labeling."

COMPETENCY 7.6 PROMOTE THE HEALTH EDUCATION PROFESSION

7.6.1 Develop a Personal Plan for Professional Growth and Service

Title Completing a Variety of Professional Development Activities

Objective The student will be able complete three activities from a variety of professional growth opportunities.

Directions

1. Discuss with the instructor types of professional growth and service for health educators in various health education settings.
2. In **Table 7.6.1-1**, review types of opportunities for professional growth that are available to participate in during the time period determined by the instructor.
3. Record the information needed in **Table 7.6.1-1** for each of the three professional growth experiences when completed.

Table 7.6.1-1 Opportunities for Professional Growth of Health Educators

Types of Opportunities	Brief Explanation of Activity Completed	Date(s) Participating in Activity	Contribution to Professional Growth Experience
Conference or workshop attended			
Webinar watched			
Book chapter or book read			
Journal article read			
Participated in school-based event			
Participated in community event			

(continues)

Table 7.6.1-1 Opportunities for Professional Growth of Health Educators *(continued)*

Attended campus-wide speaker event			
Watched television documentary			
Shadowed a health educator for 1 day			
Other (with approval of instructor)			

7.6.2 Describe State-of-the-Art Health Education Practice

Title The Competency Skills Skills Behind the Responsibilities

Objective The student will be able to describe applications of competency-based skills in various settings.

Directions

1. Review Responsibilities and Competencies of Health Education Specialists available from the site of the National Commission For Health Education Credentialing, Inc. See **Student Resource** for the URL.
2. Choose one of the seven responsibilities to record in **Table 7.6.2-1**.
3. Select any two competencies described for the chosen responsibility, then identify each in **Column 1**.
4. Identify for each competency only one sub-competency and add to **Column 2**.
5. Consider different settings such as educational institutions, hospitals, and other community organizations in which a health education specialist may work, then choose and record a different setting for each competency.
6. Complete **Table 7.6.2-1** by describing an example of how a health education specialist may apply the specific skill of each sub-competency in the identified setting.

Student Resource

National Commission For Health Education Credentialing, Inc.
http://www.nchec.org
Click on the drop-down tab "Health Education Credentialing" and select "Responsibilities and Competencies."

Table 7.6.2-1 Application of Sub-Competency Skills to Different Settings

Responsibility Chosen			
Competency	Sub-Competency	Setting	Example of Skill Application
1.			
2.			

7.6.3 Explain the Major Responsibilities of the Health Education Specialist in the Practice of Health Education

Title Roles of the Health Education Specialist

Objective The student will be able to explain the major responsibilities of the health education specialist.

Directions

1. Access the United States Department of Labor Bureau of Labor Statistics' *Occupational Outlook Handbook* and the National Commission for Health Education Credentialing web page (see **Student Resources** for the URLs) to learn about the roles and responsibilities of health education specialists.
2. Define the term *health education specialist* and explain, in two to three sentences, each of the seven areas of responsibility of the health education specialist. The explanation should not merely list the sub-competencies, but it should give examples of the types of activities that a health education specialist performs. Record the findings in **Table 7.6.3-1**.

Student Resources

1. National Commission for Health Education Credentialing
   http://www.nchec.org
   Click on the "health education credentialing" tab. From the drop-down menu, select "responsibilities and competencies."
2. United States Department of Labor, Bureau of Labor Statistics. (2011). *Occupational Outlook Handbook*
   http://www.bls.gov

Table 7.6.3-1 Roles of the Health Education Specialist

Define *health educator/health education specialist*:
Describe Responsibility I:
Describe Responsibility II:
Describe Responsibility III:

Table 7.6.3-1 Roles of the Health Education Specialist *(continued)*

Describe Responsibility IV:
Describe Responsibility V:
Describe Responsibility VI:
Describe Responsibility VII:

7.6.4 Explain the Role of Health Education Associations in Advancing the Profession

Title Functions of Professional Organizations

Objective The student will be able to explain how the functions of professional associations advance the profession.

Directions
Using **Table 7.6.4-1**, explain how the functions of professional associations that are listed help to advance the profession of health education.

Student Resource
The Coalition of National Health Education Organizations
http://www.cnheo.org
This site lists member organizations and describes a detailed working agreement.

Reference
Minelli, M. J., & Breckon, D. J. (2009). *Community health education settings, roles, and skills* (5th ed., pp. 27–28). Sudbury, MA: Jones and Bartlett.

Table 7.6.4-1 Benefits of Professional Organizations to the Health Education Profession

Functions of Professional Organizations	How Does the Function Advance the Profession of Health Education?
Standards of preparation and practice	
Continuing education and professional meetings	
Professional policies, politics, and advocacy	
Research	

Adapted from Minelli, M. J., & Breckon, D. J. (2009). *Community health education settings, roles, and skills* (5th ed., pp. 27–28). Sudbury, MA: Jones and Bartlett.

7.6.5 Explain the Benefits of Participating in Professional Organizations

Title Benefits of Joining and Participating in Health Education Organizations

Objectives
1. The student will be able to explain the benefits of membership in professional organizations.
2. The student will be able to explain the benefits of participation in professional organizations.

Directions
1. Read the article listed in **Student Resources**. This article can be found using the library search engine. Also read three additional sources on heath education professional organizations.
2. Use **Table 7.6.5-1** for **Steps 3** and **4**.
3. Describe benefits to the health educator with membership in professional organizations.
4. List types of active participation that a health educator can do in professional organizations. Give a short explanation why they are a benefit to the health educator.

Student Resources
1. Mata, H., Latham, T. P., & Ransome, Y. (2010). Benefits of professional organization membership and participation in national conferences: Considerations for students and new professionals. *Health Promotion Practice*, *11*, 450–453. doi: 10.1177/1524839910370427
2. The Coalition of National Health Education Organizations
http://www.cnheo.org

Table 7.6.5-1 Benefits of Professional Organizations to Members

Benefits of membership and active participation	
References for additional sources read	1. 2. 3.
Describe four immediate benefits of becoming a member in professional organizations (national, state or local).	1. 2. 3. 4.
List four different ways that a member can be actively involved in professional organizations. For each type of participation listed, explain how an entry-level health educator can grow professionally.	1. 2. 3. 4.

7.6.6 Facilitate Professional Growth of Self and Others

Title Facilitating Professional Growth of Others

Objective The student will be able to describe how others have facilitated another's professional growth.

Directions

1. Read the following *scenario*.
   Assume the current role of a student enrolled in an undergraduate health education major program. Reflect upon the meaning of professional growth and to what extend professional growth has been occurring from attending the first major class to date.
2. Read the instructor's handout on guidelines for writing a paper on how others have facilitated professional growth of one student.
3. Identify university faculty members or health educators who were instrumental in facilitating needed areas of personal professional growth for becoming a health educator. Give fictitious names to those identified.
4. Discuss the setting and how each faculty member or health educator assisted or facilitated professional growth. Settings include individual student–teacher conferences, seminars, classroom course work, required out-of-classroom assignments, volunteer experiences, internships/professional practice, honor student projects, club activities, leadership roles, and others.
5. Conclude by describing the following:
   a. Areas of professional growth still needing attention
   b. Ways to achieve that growth before graduation or first year of employment

Student Resource

Handout provided by the instructor on requirements of writing a paper for this activity

7.6.7 Explain the History of the Health Education Profession and Its Current and Future Implications for Professional Practice

Title Past, Present, and Future of the Health Education Profession

Objectives
1. The student will be able to explain the history of the health education profession.
2. The student will be able to discuss current and future implications for professional practice.

Directions
1. Read about the history of the health education profession. Use the resources listed in **Student Resources** and material provided by the course instructor to complete this activity.
2. Using **Table 7.6.7-1**, list the events that took place in each decade that had an impact on the health education profession and explain the implications of these events for today and the future of the profession.

Student Resources
1. Allegrante, J. P., Airhihenbuwa, C. O., Auld, M. E., Birch, D. A., Roe, K. M., & Smith, B. J., National Task Force on Accreditation in Health Education. (2004). Toward a unified system of accreditation for professional preparation in health education: Final report of the National Task Force on Accreditation in Health Education. *Health Education and Behavior, 31*(6), 668–683. doi: 10.1177/1090198104269382
2. Johnson, J. A. & Breckon, D. J. (2007). Evolution of health education, health promotion, and wellness programs. In: J. A. Johnson & D. J. Breckon, *Managing health education and promotion programs leadership skills for the 21st century* (pp. 1–25, 2nd ed.). Sudbury, MA: Jones and Bartlett. Available at http://www.jblearning.com
In the search box, type "Managing Health Education and Promotion Programs." Chapter 1 is available under "samples."
3. The National Commission for Health Education Credentialing, Inc. (NCHEC)
http://www.nchec.org
Click on "health education credentialing."
The NCHEC discusses the history of health education in the United States.

Table 7.6.7-1 Current and Future Implications of Key Events in the Health Education Profession

Decades	Events that Had (or May Have) an Impact on the Health Education Profession	Implications for Today and the Future of the Health Education Profession
1970–1979		
1980–1989		
1990–1999		
2000–2009		
2010–2019		
2020–2029		

Adapted from Johnson, J. A., & Breckon, D. J. (2007). *Managing health education and promotion programs leadership skills for the 21st century* (2nd ed., pp. 1–25). Sudbury, MA: Jones and Bartlett.

4. Bureau of Labor Statistics
http://www.bls.gov
In the search box, type "21–1091 health educators."
This document provides an overview of current employment of health educators.

5. Taub, A., Birch, D. A., Auld, M. E., Lysoby, L., & King L. R. (2009). Strengthening quality assurance in health education: Recent milestones and future directions. *Health Promotion Practice, 10*(2), 192–200. doi: 10.1177/1524839908329854

Reference

Johnson, J. A., & Breckon, D. J. (2007). *Managing health education and promotion programs leadership skills for the 21st century* (2nd ed., pp. 1–25). Sudbury, MA: Jones and Bartlett.

7.6.8 Explain the Role of Credentialing in the Promotion of the Health Education Profession

Title How Credentialing Promotes the Health Education Profession

Objectives
1. The student will be able to explain how becoming a certified health educator promotes the health education profession.
2. The student will be able to compare how accredited institutions offering a degree in health education promote the profession of health education.

Directions
1. Review the handout provided by instructor on terminology used in this activity.
2. Use **Table 7.6.8-1** to describe how each of the three components of the certified health educator credential promotes the profession.
3. Read the two articles listed in **Student Resources**.
4. Using **Table 7.6.8-2**, describe how each of the approval or accreditation possibilities promotes the profession.
5. Write a short summary explaining how credentialing individuals and universities promotes the practice of the health education profession.

Student Resources
1. Handout on terminology and acronyms provided by instructor
2. Allegrante, J. P., Airhihenbuwa, C. O., Auld, M. E., Birch, D. A., Roe, K. M., & Smith, B. J., National Task Force on Accreditation in Health Education. (2004). Toward a unified system of accreditation for professional preparation in Health Education: Final report of the National Task Force on Accreditation in Health Education. *Health Education and Behavior, 31*(6), 668–683. doi: 10.1177/1090198104269382
3. Taub, A., Birch, D. A., Auld, M. E., Lysoby, L., & King L. R. (2009). Strengthening quality assurance in health education: Recent milestones and future directions. *Health Promotion Practice, 10*(2), 192–200. doi: 10.1177/1524839908329854

Table 7.6.8-1 Promoting the Health Education Profession by Individual Certification

Components of Certified Health Educator	How Does Each Component of Health Educator Certification Promote the Profession of Health Education?
1. Academic preparation: major or degree in health education, or 25 semester hours (37 quarter hours) preparation in the seven areas of responsibility	
2. Pass the written exam	
3. Obtain a minimum of 75 continuing education credit hours for every 5-year period.	

Table 7.6.8-2 Promoting the Health Education Profession by Credentialing Institutions

Approval or Accreditation Groups	How Does Each of These Promote the Profession of Health Education?
1. Society for Public Health Education/American Association for Health Education (SOPHE/AAHE) baccalaureate program approval committee (SABPAC)	
2. Council on Education for Public Health (CEPH)	
3. The National Council for Accreditation of Teacher Education (NCATE)	
4. Teacher Education Accreditation Council (TEAC)	

7.6.9 Engage in Professional Development Activities

Title Continuing Education Requirements for Certified Health Education Specialists

Objectives
1. The student will be able to describe the continuing education requirements for the Certified Health Education Specialist.
2. The student will be able to explore continuing education opportunities for a Certified Health Education Specialist.

Directions
1. Go to the National Commission for Health Education Credentialing (NCHEC), Inc., website (see **Student Resource**) and read the continuing education FAQs.
2. Write a paper summarizing the continuing education requirements for a Certified Health Education Specialist. Describe the following:
   a. What makes a continuing education opportunity a Category 1 or Category 2
   b. How to find Certified Health Education Specialists-approved activities
   c. What the fees are for continuing education
   d. How to document and submit an attended activity
   In the paper, describe some of the activities that would be of interest, including topic, length, site, cost, and number of contact hours earned if completed.
3. Search the web for continuing education opportunities that are approved for Certified Health Education Specialists by NCHEC.

Student Resource
The National Commission for Health Education Credentialing
http://www.nchec.org
To read the continuing education FAQs, click on the FAQs button and scroll to Continuing Education.

7.6.10 Serve as a Mentor to Others

Title Benefits of Mentoring a Student or Colleague

Objective The student will be able to describe the benefits of mentorship.

Directions

1. Conduct a literature search on health education mentorship programs using ERIC online or at the school library. Click the box to view a list of peer-reviewed literature. Choose at least three full-text articles discussing the benefits and opportunities for mentorship.
2. Write a two- to three-page paper describing the benefits of mentorship, including:
   a. Definitions of mentor and mentee
   b. Benefits to the mentor
   c. Benefits to the mentee
   d. How being a mentor benefits the profession of health education
   e. Programs at the university that offer opportunities to mentor others
3. Cite sources of information in the body of the paper and include a reference page.

Student Resource

Handout provided by instructor on key words to use when searching for mentorship readings

7.6.11 Develop Materials that Contribute to the Professional Literature

Title Writing a Letter to the Editor in a Professional Journal

Objective The student will be able to describe the requirements for writing a letter to the editor for selected peer-reviewed journals.

Directions

1. Choose three journals from the following list: *Journal of the American Public Health Association, Journal of the American Dietetic Association, American Journal of Public Health, Journal of School Health, Journal of the American Medical Association*, or *Health Education and Behavior*.
2. Read one letter to the editor or commentary from each of the journals chosen in **Step 1**.
3. For each of the three journals chosen in **Step 1**, review the requirements of the journal that must be met before any submitted letter to the editor would be considered for inclusion in that journal. Examples of requirements include the length of the letter, submission timeline, and number of references allowed.
4. Prepare a PowerPoint presentation (or similar format presentation) that includes:
   a. Names of the three selected journals
   b. Purpose(s) of writing a letter to the editor identified from the three readings in **Step 2**
   c. Requirements/guidelines for writing a letter to the editor for each of the three selected journals reviewed in **Step 3**
   d. Similarities and differences of the requirements among the three journals

Student Resource

Goldman, K. D., & Schmalz, K. J. (2000). Op to it! Writing op-ed columns. *Health Promotion Practice, 1*(4), 302–304. doi: 10.1177/152483990000100402

7.6.12 Engage in Service to Advance the Health Education Profession

Title Choosing a Service Activity

Objectives
1. The student will be able to identify service activities that will advance the health education profession.
2. The student will be able to produce a video to promote service to the health education profession as a way to recruit new students to the major.

Directions
1. For each category listed in **Table 7.6.12-1**, identify four service opportunities that a health education student can do that will advance the health education profession.
2. Develop a 2–3-minute script for a video discussing how students can be of service to the health education profession. Integrate the information listed in **Table 7.6.12-1** in the video.
3. Record the video following instructions provided by the course instructor.
4. Share the video with four health education majors.
5. Ask the four viewers questions about the video. Record their responses in **Table 7.6.12-2**.
6. Modify the content of the video based upon feedback from the pilot. Then create a revised video and submit to the instructor. This video, accompanied by a brief explanation of its purpose, plus the skills involved in producing it, can be included in an e-portfolio to share with prospective employers.

Table 7.6.12-1 Service Opportunities that Advance the Profession

Category	Identify Service Activities
Local, state, or health education professional organizations	1. 2. 3. 4.
Local, state, or national health and human service nonprofit organizations	1. 2. 3. 4.
State or federal proposed legislation related to health	1. 2. 3. 4.

Table 7.6.12-2 Viewer Feedback from Pilot Test

Feedback Questions	Responses
Was the length of the video appropriate? If not, how could the video length be improved?	
What were the main points of the video?	
Were the main points of the video understandable? If not, how could the message be improved?	
Was the sound quality of the video appropriate? If not, how could the sound be improved?	
Was the picture quality of the video appropriate? If not, how could the picture be improved?	
Is a video an appropriate method for disseminating a message to recruit health education majors? Why or why not?	

Student Resources

1. Hardware and computer software to create and produce a video
2. Instructions from the course instructor about how to create and produce a video

Index